W9-CUA-072
VOLUME 1

Working in the 21st Century

Gender and Beyond

Judith Glass
Editor

INSTITUTE OF INDUSTRIAL RELATIONS
UNIVERSITY OF CALIFORNIA, LOS ANGELES

Institute of Industrial Relations
Publications Center
University of California
Los Angeles, CA 90024-1478
(310) 794-0393

To order copies of this publication, please phone (800) 247-6553.

ISBN 0-89215-186-2

Cover design adapted from a brochure design by Emily Telez, Telez Design
    Studio, Pasadena, CA.
Book design by Tanya Maiboroda.
Printed by Continental Graphics, Los Angeles, CA. 230

Acknowledgments

This book represents the culmination of a year of effort on the part of a committee drawn from UCLA and the wider community. I want to acknowledge their contributions to the conceptualization of this project on the dynamics of gender in the workplace and to thank them for their steadiness of purpose: Helen Astin, Antonette Cordero, Joy Frank, Emily Levine, Bea Mandel, Janice Reznik, Barbara Rosenbaum, Dawn Waring, and Karin Wittenborg.

Thanks are due also to the Alfred P. Sloan Foundation, Ms. Joan Palevsky, the Bank of America, and the Roth Family Foundation, whose financial support made the project possible.

This book stems from a conference titled *Working in the 21st Century: Gender and Beyond*, held at UCLA in December 1993. Co-sponsoring this event, which explored women's work experience as a function not only of gender, but of values and the structure of work, were the UCLA Institute of Industrial Relations (IIR), Bank of America, California Women's Law Center, UCLA Center for the Study of Women, UCLA Human Resources Round Table (HARRT), L.A. Area Chamber of Commerce, and the L.A. County Commission on Women.

Joan Gusten, IIR coordinator assistant, provided all the administrative help and attention to detail that complex events demand; and Rosalind Schwartz, director of the IIR Human Resource Management Center, gave me emotional and intellectual support throughout the year and was always available to consult. IIR editor Betsy A. Ryan, Ph.D., who shared my interest in the project, worked with unusual commitment to complete the manuscript editing within a limited time allotment. The contributions of Maryann McGuire, project coordinator; Juliana Tsao, word processor; and Evie Fingerman and Dottie Grossman, transcribers, also

JAN - 1998

helped bring the conference smoothly into print. I thank them all.

As a woman working in the late 20th century, I want our contemporary workplace problems to be confronted and resolved so that both women and men have more satisfying employment experiences in the future. It is my hope that this volume contributes to that end.

Judith Glass, Ph. D.
Coordinator of Public Programs, IIR

Foreword

In 1993, the Center for Human Resource Management at the UCLA Institute of Industrial Relations initiated a project on the dynamics of gender in the workplace as part of our overarching theme, "Anticipating the 21st Century." Centered around a series of public symposia, this project addresses public policy makers and change agents in the public and private sectors of the economy, including corporate and organizational leaders and decision-makers in various professions. By broadening and deepening our economic and social understanding of the dynamics of gender in the workplace, our hope was that this project might move us from intellect to appropriate action so that the full potential of our labor force—our human resources—can be realized.

The initial symposium, "Working in the 21st Century: Gender and Beyond," on which this book, Volume 1, is based, was held in December 1993. It provided a broad conceptualization of the confluence of gender, values, and the structure of the workplace, and featured lectures by noted scholars Joan R. Acker and Juliet B. Schor, writer and philosopher Emily Levine, and State Senator Gary K. Hart.

The changes facing the American economy and our working population now are on a scale comparable to those initiated by the Industrial Revolution of the 19th century. We are not merely dealing with the trough of a normal business cycle. Nothing less than the essential meanings of work, skill, education, authority, and family are involved. Issues of gender in the workplace are in the forefront of our need to address these changes.

Women are an increasing percentage of the American labor force. More than two-fifths of all workers now are women, and the Labor Department projects that women will account for the

WITHDRAWN

majority of labor force growth until 1995. By 1995, 80 percent of women between the ages of 25 and 44 are expected to be working. The revolutionary changes taking place encompass married women and mothers, even of young children. The 1990s will be the first decade in which a majority of mothers of children under six years of age, in families where the husband is present, will be in the labor force. In addition, working women are increasingly responsible for supporting families. By 1985, six million families were already being supported by female heads of household; that number can be expected to increase. (Source: Bureau of National Affairs, *Work & Family, A Changing Dynamic* 1986, 13-15)

Women entering the labor market have been a catalyst for raising many questions about the ways we work, the definitions of appropriate skills for specific jobs, the relevance of gender, and the subordination of our emotional, relational, and familial values to values of technocratic efficiency and workplace discipline. These issues intersect with our increasing awareness of the necessity of using *all* of our available labor force to optimal advantage if we are to remain competitive in a global economy. Clearly, we are not doing this now with respect to women, and we need to look seriously at the structure of work as well as emotional factors if we are to answer these questions adequately.

Our institutions were shaped to serve a society that no longer exists. They now perpetuate a power structure that may not be conducive to optimal socioeconomic performance and a satisfying personal life. Consequently, the project will consider the structure of work and the perpetuation of power. Whose interests are served now by the way work is defined and organized? What are the economic possibilities for, and implications of change in working hours, salary schedules, organizational hierarchy? How will new technologies impact the structure of work?

What are the interfaces between work and family as central institutions of our society? Up to now the family has been asked to absorb the brunt of the changes brought about by women entering the workforce, while the institutions of the workplace have been relatively untouched. How sacrosanct is the workplace when its demands clash with familial as well as other relational and communal needs of the workforce? Can we begin to see the structure of the workplace as a variable, not a given, in the interplay of gender, values, and work?

The search for balance between public and private life raises serious questions about who holds power in our society. There is already evidence that those who value their personal lives are unwilling to take positions of authority because of the time demands imposed on them. What does this mean for the quality and personality of our leadership now and in the future? How broadly can we deal with the reconceptualization of both of these institutions? Must the definition of success change?

Women and men at work: to what extent do issues like the glass ceiling involve gender discrimination; to what extent do they reflect differences in values? What is the meaning of a level playing field? How is the workplace affected by the social inequality of men and women in the culture in general? For example, the problem of sexual harassment in the workplace is set in the context of the power inequalities between women and men in the society at large. It will only disappear from the workplace when women and men are social equals. These questions are relevant not only to personal satisfaction at work, but to economic performance and efficient use of the workforce as well.

I am very pleased to present Volume 1 in our series, "Working in the 21st Century: Gender and Beyond," which will set a broad context for these important questions.

Judith Glass

Contents

Power, Productivity, and Participation

Possibilities for Workplace Change in the 21st Century

JOAN R. ACKER

Workplace change, spurred by management's anxiety over increasing global competition, the world-wide restructuring of capital and production, and the amazing capacities of new technology, is well underway. At multiple sites, in capitalist concerns and governmental organizations, power and participation are being reorganized by managers with interests in increasing productivity, efficiency, and profit in order to "win" the increasingly difficult competitive game. Many commentators agree that a fundamental transformation is underway—that jobs and work organizations will never be the same again.

Our changing workplaces are, without exception, gendered organizations; that is, organizations that systematically differentiate between women and men in ways that, on the whole, disadvantage white women and minority women and men. The questions I address in this chapter have to do with linkages between the gender structures of work organization and contemporary changes such as measures to increase flexibility in staffing and work processes, implementation of team-based work schemes, reduction of hierarchy, and changes in skill demands along with introduction of new technologies. First, are existing gender structures altered or maintained in the change process? Or, how do the changes affect women as compared with men? Second, does gender affect the change process itself? Could it be that gender divisions are used and recreated in the process of managing change?

1

Discussion of these questions must be tentative for a number of reasons. To begin with, current changes are tremendously complex and various, so that any attempt to talk about them in general will probably oversimplify that complexity. And changes are rapid, so that observations made today may not be quite right tomorrow. For example, while I was preparing this chapter, two of the organizations I planned to use as examples of a positive change scenario announced drastic staffing cuts, calling into question the seriousness of management's interest in employee involvement and commitment as the road to increased productivity.

Another problem is that the research available is not voluminous, does not cover all the possible permutations of gender and workplace change, and does not tell us how extensive the process is. Nevertheless, there are enough accounts to allow some informed speculation about what is going on now and what is apt to happen in the near future. I base my discussion on studies and observations in the U.S. and Scandinavia, including my own research in Sweden. Of course, linear extrapolations of present practices into the future are dangerous, and social scientists often make fools of themselves when they try to predict. However, I think there are a few signposts pointing to contradictory possibilities for the future.

THE GENDER STRUCTURE OF CONTEMPORARY ORGANIZATIONS

Contemporary capitalist societies and the work organizations that keep them functioning contain a fundamental division of labor between women and men. This division of labor crosses the boundaries of paid work and domestic life; it is symbolically reinforced in our movies, magazines, and advertising. It is central to our private sexual lives and to individual and group identity. This division of labor, and the meanings attached to it, are dynamic and constantly changing, but they do not disappear.[1]

In the development of capitalist economies, the work organizations that emerged were invented, owned, and controlled by powerful men in societies in which a gender division of labor and the subordination of women already existed.[2] White middle and

2

upper class women were generally excluded from these organizations, while working class women were often hired for the lowest paid labor. As a wage became more and more necessary for survival and as new kinds of clerical and service jobs emerged, women often worked for pay, but they were not the family "breadwinners"; nor were they seen as normal workers, for their place was in the home.

Women's unpaid labor was essential to the functioning of work organizations, which needed workers who were renewed each day and in each generation, but this labor was also conveniently invisible or, if visible, seen usually as outside the direct concerns of ownership and management.[3] The invisibility of the fundamental importance of unpaid domestic labor was conceptually organized through economic and management theory that focused only on the organization of production, oblivious to the organization of reproduction. Thus, "the economy" and economic organizations were justified in functioning as though people and other resources were equivalent to machines—just factors of production. The economy had a life of its own and its own goals— production and profit—that had little to do with the survival goals of individuals and families, unless fulfilling those goals could be a source of gain. This was a fundamentally gendered organization of society, built by powerful men, expressing their ways of understanding the world, and based upon a gender division of labor in which women were subordinated to men in both the home and the work organization.

In our contemporary world, although women go out to work in proportions almost as high as those of men, these fundamental gendered arrangements persist. Women are still responsible for human reproduction; economic organizations still operate with productivity and profit as overriding goals, often at the expense of individuals and families. Within organizations, gendered structures and processes still separate women and men, disadvantaging women. These structures are interconnected in real organizational life, but for analytic simplicity I want to distinguish between (1) gender hierarchies, (2) sex segregation of occupations and positions, (3) the organization of workplaces in relation to the rest of life, and (4) gender wage differences. In the remainder of this chapter, I examine how these gendered structures might be affected by the transformations underway and, conversely, how these structures may be used to facilitate and influence change processes. I focus on work organizations well aware that they are integral parts of the bigger picture of global change.

THE MAINTENANCE AND ALTERATION OF GENDER STRUCTURES

Hierarchy

Hierarchies ordered by gender are the rule in most workplaces. The higher the position on the organizational ladder, the lower the proportion of women. Women are disproportionately in the large job categories at the bottom, with routine work and little power. Images of appropriate jobs for women and men, and workplace interactions, including sexual harassment, reinforce these pervasive patterns. Internal labor markets are frequently divided into male and female sectors, with opportunity structures sharply limited in the female sector. This general structure prevails in the mid-1990s even though many women have moved into middle management and higher level professional and technical positions (Sokoloff 1992), the public consciousness of gender discrimination has greatly increased, and male managers no longer have the security they once enjoyed. All of this is well known (see Kanter 1977 and Acker 1990).

Reduction of hierarchy through the elimination of supervisors and managers and the reorganization of work processes is a primary strategy in restructuring. Some theorists have speculated that reduction of hierarchy is a precondition for greater equality between women and men (Kanter 1977; Acker 1989). Does reduction of hierarchy as it is occuring now actually improve the situations of women at work? The answer is sometimes yes, sometimes no, and sometimes yes and no, depending on how reductions in hierarchy are achieved and work is reorganized.

Some evidence exists that, given that skills and tasks are the same, a flat organization is more woman-friendly than a hierarchical one (Bielby and Baron 1986). For example, one study of professional engineers found that women have greater opportunity to use their skills and to participate on equal grounds with men in flat organizations than in hierarchical, bureaucratic ones (Kvande and Rasmussen 1990, 1994). The researchers compared matched pairs of women and men engineers in six organizations that differed in work organization and structure. In dynamic network engineering organizations, work was organized to adapt rapidly to changing markets and technologies. Power was decentralized and everyone working on a project participated in decision making. In this situation, the abilities of women were as visible as those of men, and managerial opportunities emerged out of the ongoing work. As full and visible participants, women were as likely as men to be chosen for leadership positions. In addition, in these flat organizations managers functioned as coordinators in networks rather than as leaders with followers. Women who became managers did not have to adapt to masculine stereotypes of leadership.

In contrast, in the static bureaucracies, a centralized decision making and task allocation process restricted opportunities for collaborative work and creative problem solving. Women engineers were less visible and had fewer opportunities to demonstrate professional competence than their male colleagues. Career progression was through promotion in the hierarchy, and, as many other studies have shown, there was a propensity for male managers to choose others like themselves (men) for new managerial posts. In addition, in these bureaucratic organizations, male professionals saw their women colleagues as somewhat illegitimate competitors, unfairly advantaged by affirmative action efforts. These perceptions added to the barriers to both collegiality and promotion the women experienced.

Reduction of hierarchy may increase equality for some professional and technical women while doing little for other managerial women or for women farther down in the organizational class structure. A case in point is a large West Coast communication company, employing a high proportion of women, that began in the early 1990s to restructure to decrease hierarchy and create a team problem-solving approach to better utilize employee skills. In the initial plans, reduction of hierarchy necessitated the elimination of 4,000 management jobs, to be done through attrition and early retirements. Many of the regular functions of the company were to be reorganized, and previously routine, closely supervised jobs were to become more autonomous and skilled.

For example, customer service operations were to be redesigned with the active participation of employees to increase the complexity, responsibility, autonomy, and efficiency of the work (U.S. Congress, Office of Technology Assessment 1993). The remaining professional and managerial staff in customer services would supply consultation and continual learning for other staff or would be involved in teams working on particular problems. Some jobs at the lowest level of the organization involving routine computer-aided work would not be reorganized, and employees at this level would not be part of the new participatory effort.

In September 1993 the company announced that its continuing re-engineering process would involve elimination of another 9,000 jobs (*CWA News* 1993). In published reports it was unclear how many customer service jobs had actually been restructured. The union estimates that many of the lost positions will be the very customer service jobs that had been part of the effort to increase efficiency and reduce hierarchy. Thus, the consequences of reduction of hierarchy along with the creation of more challenging jobs in collaborative settings are decidedly mixed in this case.

Reduction of hierarchy through the elimination of supervisors and middle management is often accomplished through pushing some supervisory and managerial functions downward in the organization, increasing the responsibility of lower level jobs (Smith 1990). This happened in Swedish banks in the late 1980s (Acker 1991, 1994a) as tellers, mostly women, were transformed into new customer service employees with responsibilities that had formerly been the province of managers, such as approving loans, handling foreign currency transactions, and giving advice to customers. Computer technology was designed to assist these newly skilled employees rather than to deskill them (see also Baran 1990). The women whose work was upgraded found their jobs immensely more interesting and challenging. They also experienced increased stress and much longer working hours, often uncompensated, as they used their evenings and weekends to do the studying necessary to carry out the new functions. Intensification of work for those at the bottom was one result of work restructuring and upgrading.

Centralization of managerial decisions often accompanies the reduction of hierarchy and decentralization (Smith 1990, 1993a). As middle managers disappear, control at the top, facilitated by new computer systems, may become more direct and immediate. As a consequence, reduction of hierarchy may mean less flexibility and autonomy rather than more for the remaining middle and lower level workers. Moreover, removing one or two levels of managers and supervisors also drastically limits already scarce promotion possibilities.

These contradictory consequences of reducing hierarchy affect men as well as women, but the effects may differ by gender. For example, reduction of hierarchy through flexible specialization or the development of multiskilled workers in team-organized, market-responsive production systems is likely to be a strategy for firms in which skilled male workers already predominate (Jenson 1989; Smith 1993a). Firms and functions in which women predominate are more likely to achieve hierarchy reduction through computerization of work and deskilling. Yet my examples show that this often involves management choice and that stereotypical women's jobs can become more complex and skilled—that women can benefit from reduced hierarchy.

Although men suffered higher unemployment than women as manufacturing jobs were eliminated, women are likely to be more adversely affected in the future. Women are the most recent entrants into the world of management, so they may well be disproportionately those who are the first to lose their jobs as corporations continue downsizing at administrative and managerial levels. As middle management jobs disappear, there will be fewer opportunities for the ambitious woman (or man) to move up. Minorities are also likely to be adversely affected. Women-predominant jobs in organizations, such as clerical services, have always had only a few rungs in their promotion ladders, and transfers to different and men-predominant work, such as transfers from clerical to management positions, have been difficult in most firms. Flattening of hierarchies could have a doubly negative effect on women, as their promotion prospects in their own specialities decline and as men become even more protective of the jobs they have traditionally dominated.

In sum, the changes underway in work organization hierarchies and the accompanying work restructuring have mixed implications for the future of gender structures. The general reduction of hierarchy also reduces gender hierarchy, and team-based, collaborative work may improve the chances that women will be assessed on their performance, not on their gender. Even those below professional and managerial levels may have more interesting and challenging work to do in team settings in which they experience considerable participation in decision making. On the other hand, reduction of hierarchy also means that many people lose their jobs. In addition, reduction of hierarchy can also mean that work becomes controlled more by computers than by human supervisors, but directly under the surveillance of higher level managers (Smith 1990). In these circumstances, hierarchy and power are not really reduced so much as centralized. These changes are also likely to result in new hierarchies among women, as some women have new access to power and participation, while the mass of women are deskilled and/or turned into contingent workers.

Sex Segregation of Occupations and Positions

Women are clerical workers, nurses, and nursing aides; men are carpenters, doctors, and emergency medical technicians. Sex-typing and sex segregation of jobs is a horizontal as well as a vertical feature of most work organizations. Although women have entered some formerly white male professional and technical jobs (Reskin and Roos 1990; Sokoloff 1992), only a small proportion of men and women work in identical jobs in the same workplaces (Bielby and Baron 1986; Acker 1991), so that organizations are considerably more segregated than the occupational data indicate. Moreover, there is considerable evidence that as substantial numbers of women enter a predominantly male field, men are on their way out, and new patterns of segregation emerge within the occupation (Reskin and Roos 1990). At the lower levels of organizations, whether in blue collar, white collar, or service jobs, horizontal sex segregation remains high.

The effects of restructuring on this type of horizontal job segregation within organizations has been little studied. Cockburn's (1983, 1985) studies show that, in a variety of organizations, as new technology was introduced and work was reorganized, men continued to control the technology and the better jobs. She found no decrease in sex-typing and segregation, although the reorganization of work that accompanied new technology could have provided the opportunity for change. On the contrary, control of technology along with the belief that technological skill is a male trait continued to provide the basis for male collegiality and the collective affirmation of masculinity. Femininity, and women workers, were defined as "other": without technical skill and less competent than men.

The definition of women-predominant jobs as unskilled and the devaluation of particular skills, such as those needed for nurturing or caring jobs, is pandemic in work organizations (Acker 1989; England 1992). Devaluation is built into hierarchical structures and horizontal patterns of segregation (Acker 1989). For example, in many organizations, attributions of importance and complexity of the job are congruent with the hierarchical level at which it is placed, regardless of actual skill levels required by the work. However, at any particular level, men-predominant jobs are usually defined as more skilled and responsible than women-predominant jobs.

Restructuring of work that reduces hierarchy and increases job complexity and the levels of skill and knowledge needed to do the job adequately might, in some cases, mitigate the negative effects of sex-typing on women's jobs. However, the research I have done on Swedish banks does not make me optimistic. There, as women-predominant jobs began to require more skill, knowledge, and commitment, the status of these jobs did not rise. Using relative wages within bank organizations as an indicator of relative status, the standing of these women's jobs in fact fell as new high-wage jobs in the world of international finance were created and as employers attempted to recruit and retain men in a tight labor market.

As employers seek greater flexibility in competitive markets, they also often create a new kind of horizontal segregation in workplaces. This is segregation between full-time, regular workers and part-time, temporary, and contract workers (Acker 1992b; Jenson 1989; Smith 1993a). Contingent work takes many forms, involving new sorts of workplace relationships, not easily captured in broad generalizations. For example, contract workers, although "contingent" within a firm, may be regular employees of the contracting firm (Smith 1993b). Such workers face new and challenging work relations as they answer to and mediate between the demands of two organizations.

On the whole, contingent workers have less security, fewer benefits, less chance of promotion, and lower incomes than regular, permanent workers. Temporary and part-time workers are disproportionately women (Callaghan and Hartmann 1991), and employers consciously attempt to recruit women whom the employers can define as only wanting contingent work.

Many commentators point to the development within firms of a core of multiskilled permanent employees and a periphery of relatively unskilled contingent workers (Smith 1993a; Wood 1989). Temporary workers sometimes work side by side with permanent workers, but at lower wages. For example, at a very successful electronics firm in my town, work is organized in teams, workers are multiskilled and flexible, and productivity has risen dramatically with restructuring. Flexibility is further maintained with temporary workers who are recruited on the understanding that they want temporary work because they have other interests and obligations, that they will never be regular employees, and that they accept lower wages and no benefits. When they work, it is on the assembly line with the experienced and multiskilled regular workers. Sometimes these regular workers see the temporaries as more trouble than they are worth. Almost all of the temporaries and regulars are women; thus a kind of stratification develops between women blue-collar workers.

In sum, none of the changes toward the new workplace of the 21st century seems likely to alter the contours of horizontal occupational segregation and job segregation within workplaces. Although women do enter men-predominant occupations, reorganization and resegregation of such jobs often occur (Reskin and Roos 1990). New differentiations of part-time, temporary, and contract workers from permanent core workers create new horizontal as well as vertical lines of segregation between women as well as between women and men. One contradictory possibility should be noted. If there is no long-term opening of new jobs for those millions of men who would have gone into industrial production jobs in earlier generations, young men could begin to choose women-predominant areas of work, and the gender structure of certain workplaces might tip from female to male. Bank tellers, to the extent they still exist, might once again be men; the proportion of male nurses might increase; flight attendants might become primarily men. This outcome is unlikely, since the historical record shows few changes in the direction of men moving into previously women-typed jobs, but it is possible.

The Organization of Workplaces in Relation to Life

Work in industrial societies has in the past been organized on assumptions about workers and relations between the workplace and life outside. These assumptions include, first, the notion that work is the first priority for workers; second, that it is normal and desirable for people to spend the best hours of the day and the best days of a lifetime in work organizations; third, that home and family life should adapt to the organization's demands; fourth, that the worker is a man whose daily needs are cared for outside of work, probably by a woman (Acker 1990); and fifth, that women are non-workers, or atypical and naturally flexible workers. These assumptions form the ideological grounds for the daily structuring of gender differences in organizational practices and the home.

Workplace rules reflect these assumptions in prescriptions that workers should arrive at a certain time, stay at work for prescribed periods, not bring children or other dependent relatives with them, not breastfeed babies on the job, and not spend work time solving family problems.

As women have entered the workforce in increasing proportions, the problems following from these assumptions have become clear. Except for those who think that women should go home again, almost everyone recognizes that women face severe disadvantages because of these assumptions. The need for day care, provisions for other care needs, parental leave, job protection for those who must do the caring work, and flexibility of working time are finally getting some public attention. However, although some slight progress has been made (e.g., the passage of the Family and Medical Leave Act), very little has been done to alleviate the undue stress placed upon families and life to adapt to the demands of work organizations. The *Wall Street Journal* (June 21, 1993), for example, recently documented "so much talk, so little action" in the area of work and family programs. To the extent that any effective programs are being implemented, it is probably for higher level, core workers and not for the great majority of lower paid employees, and certainly not for the part-time or temporaries.

Contemporary changes are likely to make the management of the interface between work and life more difficult. Raising skill levels, multiskilling, and reorganizing work on team and collaborative bases increases responsibility and work intensity. In the study of women and men engineers (Kvande and Rasmussen 1994) described earlier, the women who prospered in the dynamic networks were like their male colleagues—extremely competent high producers willing to work exceedingly long hours. In my bank study in Sweden (Acker 1991, 1994a), the women who most successfully made the transition to the new, multiskilled customer service worker spent much of their free time gaining new knowledge. All of them were mature women with a minimum of 15 years experience in banking and no young children.

Other studies show that reduction of hierarchy and the downward reorganization of supervisory tasks may result in work intensification as the new teams absorb the duties of their departed supervisors. Team work itself, while it has many positive results, also creates new pressures as the team comes to depend on all its members to keep work flowing smoothly (see Barker 1993). The member who takes time off—for example, a new mother—may be seen as a poor team member. Pressure can be considerably heightened where, as in the electronics firm I discussed earlier, employees are partially evaluated on the basis of their co-workers' evaluations of their team participation. Where downsizing and layoffs are underway, as is so frequent now, the pressures to prioritize work over family are only increased. This does not have to be the outcome of moving to team-organized work, however. The numbers of team members can be increased to accommodate the new tasks and the inevitable absences from work or to allow reductions in the length of the normal working day, which can mitigate the effects of increased work intensity. This has occured in some places in the Swedish public sector, but such a strategy, of course, undermines the goal of cost savings that often lies behind this reorganization of work.

Organizations frequently externalize the costs and organizational problems of dealing with workers whose family needs intrude into the workplace. Contingent workers of all kinds make this possible; workers with too many family obligations are part-time and temporary, and the underlying gender ideology is undisturbed. This is as true in Sweden as in the U.S., and the Swedish story should be cautionary for us.

Sweden has done more than any other society to institute social policies that recognize the family responsibilities of both women and men. However, in reality, women are the primary users of these programs; they take most of the parental leave, they reduce their working hours when their children are young, and they continue to work part-time in order to devote themselves to their families. Male careers are, on the whole, different from female careers. An ideology and a practice in which there are two types of workers has been institutionalized (Acker 1992, 1994b; Hirdman 1987). Of course, there are many women professionals and managers, but aside from the political sector, the representation of women in higher positions in Sweden is no greater than in the U.S., and the proportion of women working part-time is much higher. Many Swedes are well aware that equality for women in workplaces depends on the willingness of men to participate equally at home, but work organizations have done little to facilitate this. The proportions of such men may be growing (Nilssen 1992), but against this trend is the tremendous contemporary emphasis on competition, productivity, and market success that leads disproportionate numbers of young men away from commitments to the welfare state, and probably makes it more difficult for them to disregard career in favor of family.

In sum, in the U.S., work organizations have not adapted to the non-work lives of their employees, and there is no reason to think that anything that is happening now will change that situation. On the contrary, the changes of today push in the opposite direction. The dark side of participative work schemes is that they require tremendous commitment of time and energy—not flexibility to meet family needs as they arise. Team organization can be a tool for saving money by intensifying work and eliminating supervisors, but savings are rarely used to support services to lessen the burden of home responsibilities. Should the demand for labor increase and budgets in the public sector rise, more plans for family-oriented programs might be supported, but these would probably be for core, not contingent, workers.

Wage Setting and Wage Levels

The wage gap between women and men is part of the gender structure of work, produced in decision-making practices in work organizations, and helping to recreate sex segregation and hierarchical gender ordering. Studies stimulated by the comparable worth movement have greatly increased our knowledge about how this happens (Acker 1989, 1991; England 1992; Steinberg 1992), showing how gender-based wage inequality is reproduced in job evaluation and other wage setting technologies. Some progress toward wage equality has occurred as a consequence of comparable worth efforts (Hartmann and Sorensen 1994), but that progress is likely to be halted and undermined by the restructuring underway, although one might say that restructuring has contributed to gender wage equality in a perverse way: the elimination of high-wage manufacturing jobs and the transfer of some of these jobs to low-wage areas of the world affected men-predominant jobs first, and as a consequence of falling male incomes, the wage gap between women and men declined by a few percentage points in the 1980s (*The Wage Gap*, 1993).

Different consequences may follow from new wage setting approaches that some believe (e.g., Schuster and Zingheim 1992) will increase productivity and stimulate creativity through performance rather than job-based compensation systems.[4] Performance-based systems replace the job-based systems on which the comparable worth strategy was built. In job-based systems, wages are paid for the knowledge, skills, complexity of problem solving, and level of responsibility required in a job. Job incumbents are assumed to carry out the tasks at an adequate level of competence. Women-predominant jobs can be compared with men-predominant jobs with similar levels of job demands, and, if these comparable jobs have different levels of pay, adjustments can be made to achieve "comparable worth." Once performance or productivity enters the assessment, comparable worth may be much more difficult to define.[5]

If wage setting is based on individual performance, unarticulated gender stereotypes may bias assessments against the interests of women. For example, at the end of the 1980s in Swedish banks (Acker 1991) greater proportions of salary increases were allocated to individuals rather than across the board. I found this change to be associated with a growing wage gap between women and men. In general, wage setting that aims to achieve equality across broad categories of jobs probably benefits women and minority men, while individualized wages benefit white men, particularly middle and upper middle class men.

If performance-based wages are calculated on the basis of group or team productivity, women might still be disadvantaged. Women and minority men are often the majority of employees in organizational units with relatively low productivity or in units for which productivity is difficult to measure, such as day care centers or nursing homes, which are also notoriously low-wage enterprises. White men are more apt to work in high value-added enterprises, where productivity can be measured and where there may be resources for higher pay.

Swedish banks again provide an example. Local retail bank offices were largely staffed by women. Office productivity, measured in total activity, size of accounts, and loan activity, varied widely, depending on location; offices in working class neighborhoods in small towns were less profitable than centrally located large city branches. Productivity was even higher in bank units that handled international trading and large corporate accounts. A scheme to reward branch and office productivity was being tried in some banks. These schemes would allot higher raises to those units that had been more productive. Over time, the women-predominant branches in out-of-the-way places would sink farther and farther below other units.

Of course, increasing use of temporary workers and contracting out of organizational functions undermine collective efforts for wage equality, as these practices are intended to do. They create new two-tier wage systems in which members of the bottom tier have even less power to affect their wages and other conditions of employment than do those in the top tier.

In sum, organizations are changing wage-setting systems as they are attempting to become lean and mean. To the extent that old, stable bureaucratic systems are undermined, recent strategies for wage equity are also undermined. There is no indication that new systems might contain less gender bias than the old systems and no indication of awareness of such problems by those proposing new systems. Indeed, new systems may result in increased influence of gender stereotypes on wage setting practices, particularly if these systems base wages on individual performance.

DOES GENDER AFFECT THE CHANGE PROCESS?

Perhaps one reason that gender structures seem to be reorganized rather than eliminated in the process of restructuring is that gender continues to be useful to the powerful. I believe that gender has long been, and is today, a resource for managers in maintaining organizational viability, achieving flexibility, and managing organizational change. Gender-based job segregation within organizations often preserves low wage levels for sizeable proportions of the workforce, resulting in considerable savings on wages, while allowing higher wages to be paid to some workers who are thought to have particular skills. In industry, for example, where women are employed it is often in repetitive assembly or machine tending jobs, while men repair machines, maintain the facilities, and do other skilled production tasks (Baude 1992). Such gender divisions often facilitate staffing flexibility in portions of the labor force while allowing employers to maintain a desired core of regular, permanent workers. Defining the core as male and the periphery as female reduces potential conflict over who is to be retained and who is to be on call.

Gender ideology—for example, beliefs that men must earn a living wage while women do not need to, or that men are naturally adept at repairing machines while women are not—justifies these practices, as do training and recruitment methods. Stability is furthered by the ways in which individual and group gender identities are mobilized in the interest of gender differentiation at work. For example, white men have resisted the incursion of women into jobs they dominate partly on grounds that women are not fit for such work in fields such as printing (Cockburn 1983; Baran 1990) and forestry (Enarson 1984). Gender ideology may also facilitate a reorganization of work processes and the introduction of new technology in which high priced male labor is replaced by lower priced, less skilled female labor. Reskin and Roos (1990, p. 51) suggest that "employers gerrymandered the sex labels of jobs that were feminizing for other reasons, selectively invoking sex stereotypes after they decided to hire more women." These usages of gender to save on wages and achieve flexibility are not new phenomena, although some commentators identify them as particularly common in the present drive for efficiency and competitive advantage (Standing 1989; Jenson 1989; Smith 1993a).

Gender has also been a resource in corporate downsizing and managing technological change. A prime example is the downsizing of AT&T in the 1970s before the break-up of the Bell System (Hacker 1979). Following AT&T's loss of a large sex discrimination suit and the subsequent requirement that it institute affirmative action for women and minorities, women and minority men were integrated into jobs that had previously been in the white male domain. However, many of these jobs were already slated for elimination because of new technology. As these jobs were phased out and as traditional female jobs also were eliminated, the employment of women declined dramatically while the employment of men increased. Management, Hacker argues, believed that jobs with women incumbents could be easily eliminated without conflict because of high turnover and passivity of women employees. So far as I know, no comparable studies of contemporary corporate downsizing are yet available.

In today's world of downsizing and job elimination men as well as women, managers as well as workers, are affected. Perhaps gender is no longer used as a buffer to maintain organizational commitment and stability in the same way that it was in the past. However, we do not have enough information for such a generalization. It is more likely that there is great variation and that gender distinctions are there to be used when convenient. One way that gender could be used today is as an aid in the job elimination process itself. Some research has shown that women's managerial style is more people-oriented (Statham 1987) and interactive (Rosener 1990) than the style of men. People-oriented, interactive styles of management could be useful in "managing out" (Smith 1990) other employees, although people-oriented and interactive managers might themselves experience great stress when they have to get rid of others.

Gender may affect change processes in other ways. A fundamental contradiction seems to exist between the individualistic ethos of greater competition and the cooperative ethos of team-organized and flexible work relations. Women may be better able than men to function in team settings, thus serving to facilitate these transformations in some cases. I found indications of this in my study of Swedish banks (Acker 1994a). The branch office with only women staff had gone the farthest in developing team work, the multiskilled, flexible customer service worker, and the reduction of hierarchy. In contrast, in the office with the most men, the new goals had been rejected in practice, and hierarchy, specialization, and competition between subunits persisted. Team work in the woman-staffed branch was probably enhanced by lack of ambition for individual promotion. Several of these women had tried for promotion in the past, but had been rebuffed. Their individual stories made clear that opportunities had been blocked because they were women. By the time of my study they had accepted as fact that they would never move to higher positions. Lack of competitiveness enhanced cooperation. More interesting and challenging work was what they wanted, and that they achieved without promotion. Bank management benefited greatly as business expanded rapidly at little extra cost in wages.

Conclusion

The reorganization of power and participation in the interests of increased productivity and profit has contradictory implications for the gender structures of workplaces. The drive to reduce hierarchy and to increase worker participation and autonomy can greatly improve women's opportunities and the quality of their work experiences. But these positive outcomes are likely to result for only a minority, although that minority might cut across class lines, including blue-collar, white-collar, and professional and managerial women.

For most, at least at the present time, the outlook is dim. Transforming the old gender structures of work organizations is not on the agenda of most employers. The imperative to reduce costs to remain competitive militates against any reforms that cost money, such as family leaves or subsidized day care. Life still has to adapt to work, and women are the ones who still make this happen. Reduction of hierarchy may only mean centralization of decision making and control and, thus, loss of autonomy. Gender segregation and gender hierarchy are still prevalent. Flexibility for most organizations means flexibility in staffing and wage set-ting, not the development of multiskilled and commited workers. Where there is such a commitment, men are more likely than women to be the new core workers. Wage cutting, not wage eq-uity, is the order of the day. Old controls in law and collective agreements are either eroded or irrelevant in the new conditions of global competition. Gender organizes the international divi-sion of labor as well as the national and local divisions and will not soon disappear as a fundamental principle of division and control.

However, an unrealistic optimist might argue that now we have models of gender-equal work organization that could be widely used when and if the economy improves and organiza-tions no longer feel they must downsize or ship jobs to lower wage areas of the world. The optimist might also argue that tradi-tional gender arrangements that contributed to growth and stabil-ity of capitalist organizations and the capitalist system as a whole have been undermined. Traditional masculinity is threatened by the disappearance of men's manufacturing and management jobs and by women's increasing economic independence. Women are not passive and subordinate, if they ever were, and they speak out for equal rights and against discrimination. Perhaps new forms of masculinity not based on superiority over and disdain for women will emerge as work and life are organized in more egali-tarian and humane ways. Such developments would act back on the ways that gender differences inform organization. Models for that also exist.

But I am not optimistic. Increasing competition in a global-ized economy does not foster new masculinities, but encourages instead a resurgence of a 19th century, and perhaps more viru-lent, entrepreneurial spirit. This is the hegemonic masculinity (Connell 1988) of the immediate future. Men who embrace such an identity may not fear women, but they will not deflect re-sources they see as necessary for the great win in the world competitive battle to other purposes such as reducing the disad-vantage of women and the dominance of work organizations over life.

DISCUSSION

Q: Many of these men workers have also wives who work. Isn't it of benefit to them to fight for changes in equality? I mean they're penalizing themselves, really, by not asking for better conditions for their partners.

JOAN ACKER: I think you're actually right. Men with working wives are much more in favor of women's working and equality in the workplace than men with stay-at-home wives. That's clear. But then men are quite a contradiction and this has been true since the middle of the 19th century. Let's be crass. They want the income of their wives to help the family; at the same time, they don't want women to compete with them. So there is a real contradiction here. And as long as we do not have full employment (I think our unemployment is much higher than they're saying) they're going to see women as very competitive. So I don't know. Good point.

Q: The conference is called, "Working in the 21st Century," and I believe that in the 21st century multimedia, other kinds of work, working at home on electronic terminals, interactive television, etc. are really going to change the whole nature of work. And I think some of the things you're talking about are going to change with them, and I'd like to know how you feel about that.

JOAN ACKER: Well, I think that on a world basis, of course, this is only going to affect a few people. And so I'm very alarmed about that whole development because I think it's going to simply accelerate the growth of huge differences within this country as well as, as I said, on a world basis. I think that you're right that the work situation of many people will change and there might be some improvement. I even see this contingent, temporary part-time work as having a positive side in that as long as there's work, people are less under the long-term surveillance and control of bosses they may not like, or might be very unreasonable, and so forth, but the research that we have so far shows a mixed picture, again, about work in the home using computer-aided processes. Now, there's not a lot of research but it has, of course, happened, and one of the things that seems clear is that for certain professionals, it may be very good, very nice, and frees them up from a lot of the organizational hassles, but these professionals tend to be men, although they could be women, of course, as more women become these kinds of professionals. Most of the women tend to do much more routine, less skilled kinds of jobs, and of course if you're monitored through your computer as many workers are in this country, you can be monitored through your computer at home as well as monitored at work. You're right, it's going to change. Work relations are going to change for those people who are involved in this.

I want to say just one other thing about it. It may change a lot from what I'm saying now but there is an interesting study that was done in Finland on home-based work. They looked at the differences between men and women in this home-based work. What they found was that the men working at home worked just as though they were in the office. They got up in the morning and went to their computers and worked all day and I suppose took some time off for lunch and paid no attention to what was going on in the household. The women, however, structured their work around the needs of the family, and so found their time to work in the spaces where they didn't have family obligations. In other words, there was a different gender pattern that continued when the work was being done in the home. Now I'm not saying this couldn't change. It could, of course. But I'm really terribly worried about the extreme stratification that we're getting, and it's going to get worse, I think, between those who have access to this, and those who don't.

Q: This is more in the nature of a comment than a question. The family-friendly work place, I'm proud to say, is closer to reality in Los Angeles than many other places. We've been a leader in that. I take a more optimistic point of view than you do in the changes in the workplace. It wasn't very long ago when the workplace said, "Drop your family responsibilities when you enter these doors. We don't want to hear about anything that's happening in your life aside from your performance at work." That has really changed. Because we are more family-friendly. We are now more concerned with whether the childcare is okay, allowing for those calls at 3 o'clock to make sure your kids are alright, and helping find care for your aging parent. All those assistance programs are in place to do that. The Los Angeles Department of Water and Power, the most male-oriented, engineer dominated department in the city, has the most family-friendly policies of anybody, including probably the largest number of corporation-owned breast pumps in the world. No joke. Absolutely true. Beepers for prospective fathers to be beeped when the woman goes into labor. Things that carry family-friendly to a degree that some of us never anticipated. On the other hand, a lot of this needs to be carried out by middle level managers who haven't been informed that this is the way things are these days and that's where the rub comes. So it isn't easy and it isn't perfect, but I see it moving along that line at least in the public sector to a much greater degree. I don't fool myself that things are wonderful, but I do say things are improved. One last word. Pat Schroeder still says that when you're late to work it is more acceptable to say that you had a car problem than that you had a day care problem, and we've got to overcome that before things are significantly better.

JOAN ACKER: Well, I'm glad to hear something optimistic. That's great. I think the public sector is going to be a leader in this, undoubtedly because that's the sector where we can have some influence. The private sector is much more difficult to deal with on wage equity as well as on the family issues.

Q: I was just wondering whether in the 21st century, judging from what you said, we should stop working on issues of comparable worth and equal pay for equal work because you're implying that they're part of the old bureaucratic stratification structure and really not going to be good for women.

JOAN ACKER: No, I don't think we should stop working on pay equity issues. Our strategy has been based on the old bureaucratic pay systems. I think that the new pay systems could incorporate equity issues, but I'm really very much against individual-based wages, pay for productivity. I think it can only be bad for women. But I think that we need to do a lot of work thinking about new pay systems that adapt better to ways of organizing work, but at the same time do not allow this kind of gender stereotype to become a factor in wage setting. We also need to, of course, change the whole valuation of the jobs women do in a more positive direction.

NOTES

[1] A tremendous literature now exists in almost every academic discipline that describes and analyzes gender divisions and differentiations.

[2] See Kessler-Harris (1982) for a history of women and work in the United States.

[3] Historically, there are important exceptions, such as company towns and instances in which employers provided dormitories for workers, as in the early New England textile industry. Employers were concerned with reproduction when labor supply was scarce in particular places, or when they felt that stability and control of workers would be increased with employer interest in workers' families.

[4] Of course, piece rates are performance-based. Piece rate systems seem to have declined in usage, but where they still exist, they are disproportionately found in women-predominant jobs.

[5] For other criticisms of pay for performance wage setting see Kohn (1993) in the *Harvard Business Review* and the discussion of his arguments in the next number of that journal.

REFERENCES

Acker, Joan. 1989. *Doing Comparable Worth: Gender Class and Pay Equity*. Philadelphia: Temple University Press.

Acker, Joan. 1990. "Hierarchies, Jobs, Bodies: A Theory of Gendered Organizations." *Gender & Society* 4,

Acker, Joan. 1991. "Thinking About Wages: The Gendered Wage Gap in Swedish Banks." *Gender & Society* 5, 3: 390-407.

Acker, Joan. 1992a. "Gendering Organizational Theory." In *Gendering Organizational Analysis*, eds. Albert J. Mills and Peta Tancred. London: Sage.

Acker, Joan. 1992b. "The Future of Women and Work: Ending the Twentieth Century." *Sociological Perspectives* 35: 53-68.

Acker, Joan. 1994a. "The Gender Regime in Swedish Banks." *Scandinavian Journal of Management*, forthcoming.

Acker, Joan. 1994b. "Family, Gender, and Public Policy: The Swedish Case." In *The Family in Cross Cultural Perspective*, eds. Catherine Berheide and Esther Ling Chow. Albany, NY: SUNY Press, forthcoming.

Baran, Barbara. 1990. "The New Economy: Female Labor and the Office of the Future." In *Women, Class, and the Feminist Imagination*, eds. Karen V. Hansen and Ilene J. Philipson. Philadelphia: Temple University Press, 517-534.

Barker, James R. 1993. "Tightening the Iron Cage: Concertive Control in Self-Managing Teams." *Administrative Science Quarterly* 38:408-437.

Baude, Annika. 1992. *Kvinnans plats pa jobbet*. Stockholm: SNS Forlog.

Bielby, William T. and James N. Baron. 1986. "A Woman's Place is with Other Women: Sex Segregation Within Organizations." In *Sex Segregation in the Workplace: Trends, Explanations,*

Remedies, ed. Barbara F. Reskin. Washington, D.C.: National Academy Press, 27-55.

Callaghan, Polly and Heidi Hartmann. 1991. *Contingent Work: A Chart Book on Part-time and Temporary Employment.* Washington, D.C.: Economic Policy Institute/Institute for Women's Policy Research.

Cockburn, Cynthia. 1983. *Brothers: Male Dominance and Technological Change.* London: Pluto Press.

Cockburn, Cynthia. 1985. *Machinery of Dominance: Women, Men, and Technological Change.* London: Pluto Press.

Connell, R.W. 1988. *Gender and Power.* Stanford: Stanford University Press.

"CWA Leaders Fight to 'Mitigate Mess' at U.S. West." *CWA News*, October 4, 1993.

Enarson, Elaine Pitt. 1984. *Woods-Working Women: Sexual Integration in the U.S. Forest Service.* University, Alabama: The University of Alabama Press.

England, Paula. 1992. *Comparable Worth: Theories and Evidence.* Hawthorne, NY: Aldine de Gruyter.

Hacker, Sally L. 1979. "Sex Stratification, Technology and Organizational Change: A Longitudinal Case Study of AT&T." *Social Problems* 26: 539-557.

Hartmann, Heidi and Elaine Sorensen. 1994. *Pay Equity in State Governments.* Washington, D.C.: Institute for Women's Policy Research/The Urban Institute, forthcoming.

Hirdman, Yvonne. 1987. *The Swedish Welfare State and the Gender System: A Theoretical and Empirical Sketch*, English Series, Report No. 7. Uppsala: The Study of Power and Democracy in Sweden.

Jenson, Jane. 1989. "The Talents of Women, the Skills of Men:

Flexible Specialization and Women." In *The Transformation of Work?* ed. Stephen Wood. London: Unwin Hyman, 141-155.

Kanter, Rosabeth Moss. 1977. *Men and Women of the Corporation.* New York: Basic Books.

Kessler-Harris, Alice. 1982. *Out to Work: A History of Wage-Earning Women in the United States.* New York: Oxford University Press.

Kohn, Alfie. 1993. "Why Incentive Plans Cannot Work." *Harvard Business Review* 71, 5: 54-63.

Kvande, Elin and Bente Rasmussen. 1990. *Nye Kvinnelin, Kvinner i menns organisasjoner. (New Life for Women: Women in Men's Organizations).* Oslo: Ad Notam.

Kvande, Elin and Bente Rasmussen. 1994. "Men in Male Dominated Organizations and Their Encounter with Women Intruders." *Scandinavian Journal of Management,* forthcoming.

Nilsson, Arne. 1992. "Den Nye Mannen-finns han redan?" In *Kvinnors och mans liv och arbete,* Joan Acker, m.fl. Stockholm: SNS Forlog.

Reskin, Barbara and Patricia Roos, eds. 1990. *Job Queues, Gender Queues: Explaining Women's Inroads into Male Occupations.* Philadelphia: Temple University Press.

Rosener, Judy B. "Ways Women Lead." *Harvard Business Review.* November-December 1990: 119-125.

Schuster, Jay R. and Patricia K. Zingheim. 1992. *The New Pay: Linking Employee and Organizational Performance.* New York: Lexington Books.

Smith, Vicki. 1990. *Managing in the Corporate Interest.* Berkeley, CA: University of California Press.

Smith, Vicki. 1993a. "Flexibility in Work and Employment: The Impact on Women." *Research in the Sociology of Organizations,* 11: 195-216.

Smith, Vicki. 1993b. "Institutionalizing Flexibility in a Service Firm: Paradoxes and Consequences." Paper presented at the American Sociological Association meetings, Miami, August.

Sokoloff, Natalie. 1992. *Black Women and White Women in the Professions*. New York, London: Routledge.

Standing, Guy. 1989. "Global Feminization through Flexible Labor." *World Development*, 17: 1077-1095.

Statham, Anne. 1987. *The Gender Model Revisited: Differences in the Management Styles of Men and Women*, 409-429.

Steinberg, Ronnie J. 1992. "Gendered Instructions: Cultural Lag and Gender Bias in the Hay System of Job Evaluation." *Work and Occupations*, 19: 387-424.

U.S. Congress, Office of Technology Assessment. *Pulling Together for Productivity: A Union-Management Initiative at U S West, Inc.*, OTA-ITE-583. Washington, D.C.: U.S. Government Printing Office, September 1993.

The Wage Gap: Women's and Men's Earnings. 1993. Washington D.C.: Institute for Women's Policy Research.

"Work and Family." 1993. *The Wall Street Journal*, June 21: R1-R13.

Wood, Stephen. 1989. *The Transformation of Work? Skill, Flexibility and the Labour Process*. London: Unwin Hyman.

Revisioning Worktime

New Models of Employment for the 21st Century

JULIET B. SCHOR

In the last 40 years, productivity in this country has increased by a factor of roughly 2.6. Had we decided to use our productivity increase—i.e., the increase in the amount of output that each worker produces an hour, we could have reduced our worktime by just that factor. So we could today have a 20-hour week. Or we could have a 2-1/2-day week, or a 6-month year, or every worker in this country could be taking every other year off on a sabbatical—with pay.

I don't think it will be a surprise to any of you that instead of using this productivity increase—the economic progress being generated by technological change, higher standards of education, and better organizational methods—to reduce worktime, we have put all of it toward increasing the amount of output that we earn and consume. The average person in this country had no reduction in his or her working time, but had an increase in consumption by roughly that same factor—about 2-1/2.

As we know, in recent years the income distribution has gotten worse, so that the people at the bottom, particularly the bottom third, have been slipping back quite considerably in terms of their standard of living. But if we look over the longer period of the postwar era, what's very clear is that at all levels of the income distribution, people have experienced roughly more than a doubling of their income. The result is that today we face not so much a problem of our material standard of living, but rather a problem of time. I like to think of it in terms of saying we've become very rich in things and in the process have become very poor in time.

There are a number of dimensions to this. Joan Acker talked about the work/family conflict, which in many ways has become the most visible and I think the most obvious dimension of the problem of working time in this country. We are experiencing it and speaking about it mainly in terms of the strains being put on the family today as a result of the demands of the workplace. This has been thought of exclusively as a women's issue for a long time, and certainly it is very much a women's issue because, as I'll argue in a minute, I believe that the demands of the workplace in terms of time today are basically and fundamentally incompatible with major family responsibilities. That incompatibility is at the source of a lot of the problems that women are having today in terms of their careers, in particular, and their work lives in general.

It is also very much a men's issue, and it is becoming increasingly so as the gender division of labor in the household is changing in response to the new gender ideologies, changing gender roles, and changing desires by men to be more involved in the upbringing of children than were earlier generations. Further, it is very much a children's issue. I believe that while the crisis of youth in this country has many dimensions to it, the growth of working time by parents is very much at its core. The decline in the amount of time that parents have available to spend with their children has been very detrimental to the well-being of children.

It is also a quality of life issue for people who are not in conventionally defined families or for people who do not have children or have grown children. These groups are experiencing growing desires for what we might call a set of personal fulfillment goals. People are interested in pursuing things outside of work, and are articulating increasing desires for that. Community and volunteer work are an obvious casualty of the conflicts arising from the demands of the workplace, as are people's abilities to do the other things that interest them in their lives.

I also think we need to understand that for the most part we have been absolutely blind to the fact that the rise in working hours for employed people is very much at the core of the growing unemployment problem in this country. I have now come to a point of view I did not share when I began my work on worktime—that unless we do something about reducing worktime in this country, we will not be able to solve the problem of unemployment.

THE GROWTH OF WORKTIME

I want to talk about the issue of time as it relates to gender, work/family conflict, and the question of whether it is possible for us to move to a society in which working hours are significantly reduced. And that comes, in the end, to the question of feasibility, costs, and economic liability.

Let me start with a few statistics. I don't want to get bogged down in numbers, but I want to give you a picture of what's happening to what we'll call the prototypical family in the United States in terms of the hours of work that family unit is providing, both in the paid economy (that is, the market) and the household economy (that is, unpaid domestic labor, child care, cooking, cleaning up, shopping, lawn care, finances—all of the work that people do unpaid in their households). If we look at the changing hours of labor of the American household, we can see the core of the problem that we're facing today.

Just so we have a sense of how important this unpaid labor is, let me say that today there is roughly as much unpaid labor done in this society as paid labor. It's "invisible"; there are no government statistics on it. It's the hidden economy, and yet, in terms of people's time, it's roughly as important.

Let me take a family in 1969—and I can't go back earlier to the mythic 1950s because the data I'm using don't extend that far back—and compare this prototypical family with a family at the peak of the last business cycle before the recession started, a heterosexual married couple family with two children in a middle income group. Though I'm taking this as a prototype, these trends hold for lower income groups, higher income groups, and lots of other groups. I am controlling for a lot of things here to see how much work that family was doing in 1969 and at the end of the 1980s.

In 1969, the average husband in a family like this put in just under 2,300 hours a year in the paid labor market (a 40-hour-per-week job for 50 weeks a year is a 2,000-hour-per-year job.) The 40-hour week is a standard we've never achieved for full-time workers. Instead, we've remained at a 43-hour-per-week average for full-time workers. The average 1969 husband also put in about 670 hours in the family economy, that is, unpaid labor at home, for a total of just under 3,000 hours a year—quite a hefty schedule.

Now, the 1969 prototypical wife was not employed, but worked full time as a housewife. The housewife also worked very long hours. Despite a century of labor-saving technological change, housewives' hours really didn't change much over the 20th century until the mid 1970s. (In 1969, she was working roughly 2,500 hours a year as well, for a total family labor of about 5,400 hours each year in both the household and the market sphere.

It's probably not a surprise to you what happened next: women went into the paid labor force in big numbers. The number of hours they worked increased, and the number doing full-time work increased, so that "full-time housewife" now describes a much smaller fraction of total women. The labor hours of the prototypical family of the late 1980s increased quite substantially by over 1,000 hours a year, or about half a worker.

Let me say a little about the dimensions of that. The husband's market hours actually did not fall at all from 1969 to the late 1980s, which is something one would expect in a situation where the spouse is coming into the labor market doing much more paid employment. The obvious thing we might expect is that men would be moving out of the labor force a little bit more, doing more at home, and compensating in that way. But in fact, once we correct for unemployment and underemployment, men with jobs have actually increased their worktime by about 70 hours per year. So just at the moment in history when women need their husbands or their partners at home to be doing more, they are less available, because their workplaces are getting more of their time. They have increased their hours in the household economy, but not by nearly enough to compensate. They're up to about 785 hours a year, for a total of about 3,200 hours. So they've increased their total worktime hours by about 250 over this period.

Women, on the other hand, are now splitting their worktime much more between market and home. The full-time woman worker is putting in just over 2,000 hours a year in the market, but at home she's only cutting back by an average of half an hour for every extra hour she's working in the market. So she's working a little under 1,300 hours a year in the household economy as well. And I should note that I am using the most conservative statistics on household hours: there are other, less reliable statistics that indicate considerably higher hours for working women, so remember that these would be a lower-bound estimate. My average of total worktime for a full-time working woman in an intact marriage with two children in the late 1980s is about 65 hours a week. The recall method, where people are called on the phone and asked how much they're working, gives numbers closer to 85 hours a week.

In any case, the employed mother's total hours have now gone up to 3,280, and total family hours are at just under 6,500 hours a year. Women have increased by just over 800 hours a year the amount of work they're doing when they shift from full-time housewife to full-time worker. That's an increase of 1/3; very, very substantial. As we know, women have borne the bulk of the increase. Men are doing more, as well.

This is the underlying dynamic of the work/family conflict. Families are giving just over 1,000 more hours in total worktime. They're getting 1,000 fewer hours of household services, because the wife has cut back by more than 1,000; the husband hasn't increased by much, so that in terms of what's being done in the family—and remember, I'm holding constant the number of children, so we're not looking at people doing less because there are fewer children around—that's half a worker less at home to do the household work. What families are getting more of is income, but remember, it's not a full 2,000-hour-per-year extra income, because it's not a male income, so we're already lopping off 30 percent of this income. Also, the expenses associated with increased women's worktime are very high because of childcare expenses, clothing expenses, commuting expenses, and so on. So the increase in income being generated from this is not truly commensurate.

There's a lot that is positive about this. Stay-at-home housewives had a lot of difficulties. The stress and mental problems associated with full-time housewives in the Ozzie and Harriet family of the 1950s are quite serious. In terms of women's well-being, the growth in labor force participation has been a positive thing, on balance. But that does not mean it's a change without very serious problems, and I want to turn to those.

EMPLOYMENT NORMS AND GENDER

The problem of the family has been defined by the Right as that of women going out into the workplace. I think that is a very narrow-minded and wrong way to look at it. It's also an impractical view because the Right's solution is to get women back into the household, and that's not going to happen, whatever we think about it. I think we have to understand that the problem has been the structure of the paid economy that women have gone into, and the structure of jobs, and that this more than anything has been responsible for high levels of work/family conflict. Let's remember what happened when we went from a situation of a full-time household worker taking care of the household, the extended family, and the community in unpaid labor. That person is now basically absent, and we have not replaced that system with anything else. We have a patchwork system that is not working. And that is a big part of the crisis of raising children in this country—the stress that people are experiencing between work and family, the conflicts of working that out, and the problems women are having advancing in the labor market. Mental stress is now the fastest growing claim in the worker's compensation system, and also a very expensive one.

Let me turn to the employment model and the structure of jobs that women have come into. I want to describe mainly professional/managerial kinds of jobs, because I think hourly workers face a different set of issues. Though equally important (they have their own problems of long working hours), I'm going to put those aside for a minute.

Job as number one priority is very much at the center of the conception of the professional/managerial job. The employee gives up control over his or her time, essentially, in return for a lucrative salary as compared to salaries and wages across the occupational spectrum. What are the dimensions of this? I think the most important is long hours of work. A 40-hour-per-week job does not exist in professional/managerial categories unless employees are on reduced working times. We were talking earlier about lawyers; in the corporate law firms, a 40-hour schedule is the part-time schedule.

A second dimension of this is that working hours are a gray area. They are not negotiated when a person takes a job. One negotiates for a salary. There is some idea about the working hours, and if one is able to talk to future co-workers one may get a reasonable idea. But it's not something that the employer negotiates when one takes the job. What happens over time in these jobs is that the working hours tend to increase, especially as people get promotions, then of course, there's a point where they start to drop off. The CEO can take the weekend, and doesn't have to work nights. There is an end to it, but in terms of where most people are, the upward movement in jobs is associated with increases in the hours.

Third is the concept of on demand, whether it's to a supervisor (immediate or otherwise) or to a client. The idea is that the employee's time is available to be demanded by superiors or clients. Related to this is the concept of a willingness to sacrifice family time for job demands. Very frequent questions at interviews for jobs are: "Can you work nights and weekends, can you travel, are you willing to relocate, are you willing to drop family plans," and so on. Success in the job is contingent, in many ways, on the ability to sacrifice family time for the employer. There's a high correlation between promotions and the amount of time spent at work. Some people call this the "face time" syndrome; that is, the employee is supposed to be at work showing his or her face in order to give a signal of loyalty and commitment to the firm. The extent to which time at work is used as a signal to the employer—not necessarily about the content of time, but about whether the employee is willing to make the sacrifices—is very important in success. I had a conversation the other day with Ellen Goodman, the syndicated columnist, who reported that at the *Boston Globe*, when the women's group went to management with a report about the problems they were having, they called this problem the "last man standing" syndrome.

Next, there is the intensity of supervision and the nature of supervision—the idea that we have to be in face-to-face contact with our supervisors, or if we are supervisors, with the people below us, which takes away flexibility and the ability to be at home working without supervision. This has been a barrier to people who are trying to negotiate new kinds of work arrangements.

A final dimension of the professional job is connected with the promotion/hour correlation: the correlation of pay with hours and the idea that productivity is correlated with hours. The idea that people who work longer hours are the more productive, efficient employees actually goes against common sense. We could have a system in which we think that the people who can get their work done and just go home by 5:00 or 6:00 are the efficient ones, but instead we have a system in which the incentives are for people to do their work less efficiently because they don't feel they can go home anyway. The evidence does not support the idea that long hours are correlated with productivity; rather, it suggests that as hours are reduced, the intensity of work and efficiency per unit of time rises. It also suggests that in professional and managerial jobs, productivity does not correlate with number of hours, at least for the range of hours we are discussing.

So the connection between productivity, efficiency, and therefore, pay, is largely a myth. One of the things we really have to do is start thinking very hard about new systems of paying and promoting people that are not based on the "last man standing" syndrome.

In my own work I have developed an argument that the salaried worker has a particular problem vis-à-vis hours, which is that, because hours are not negotiated and one negotiates for a flat salary per year, the employer has an incentive to try and increase the number of hours that he or she gets out of the worker. That's because extra hours are not remunerated. I have found in my research that, correcting for everything else and holding constant education, income, gender, etc., merely the fact of being paid on a salary will increase hours approximately 140 hours a year. For salaried workers in particular we need to be thinking about legal protections afforded them with respect to hours, which don't exist anywhere except California. In this state some salaried workers are covered by overtime laws.

What is the evidence that this is the model of employment? There's a lot in the work/family qualitative literature on this. The other piece of more quantitative evidence we can point to is the fact that jobs in the less than 40-hour-a-week range basically don't exist for salaried workers. They mostly don't exist for other people, either, except for dead-end, part-time kinds of work. But particularly in the 20-hour to 40-hour-a-week range, there are very few people in those categories right now. And that is where more and more people are saying they want to be. There is a very serious failure of the job market to provide those kinds of worktime options for people.

I want to talk about what's wrong with this model. The key concerns are the incompatibility between working in jobs like this and reproducing families and communities, and the unemployment problem. What would new models of work look like, and how can we replace this old model—which I could call a male model of employment, because it was designed for men who had full-time support people at home? Let me start with the family-friendly firm.

Many family-friendly policies are basically designed with the following model: What can we do to make it easier for the family to adapt to the needs of the workplace? How can we make it easier for people to work long hours? How can we make it easier for them to get to work when a child is sick or when their babysitter doesn't come? How can we make it easier for them to stay longer and to get rid of the stress that they're feeling (as if it were just a stress management problem, and not something arising from something very real)? The family-friendly reforms have given us yoga classes and health clubs so we can make it through another week. They've given us day care and night care—we now have children who are in child care during the 7 a.m. to 11 p.m. shifts and even the 11 p.m. to 7 a.m. shifts. We have children who don't get to be with their parents when they're sick, but go to the workplace and stay there with strangers. Of course, it's better than having children stay at home alone, having their mothers drop out of their jobs, or having them go to school when they're sick. But I don't believe it is the right solution.

I believe we have to think about models that ask the workplace to adapt and change its expectations so as to provide an environment for bringing up children that is responsive to the needs of children and not to the needs of employers. We've gone much too far in the direction of asking the family to respond to the needs of employers. Instead, the economy needs to begin providing job scheduling options for people that allow them to actually reduce their working time. This means, particularly in the professional and managerial categories, that we must decouple the connection between hours and upward mobility and between hours and success; eliminate the use of hours as a signal or a symbol of loyalty to the corporation; and provide a variety of scheduling options that eliminate the old full-time/part-time distinction, which was based on the family wage or male breadwinner model.

We need a system that allows people much more choice of hours. Right now, the choice of hours is very largely in the purview of the employer, and people who want short-hour jobs are forced to take very severe penalties in wages, benefits, and promotion possibilities. Those penalties are way out of line with the costs to the employer or the productivity differential between workers who work long hours and short hours. We do not have a real market in hours in this country. We have negotiation about pay and virtually no negotiation about hours. And that is a serious failure in the market that we need to address on a number of dimensions.

Because we're talking about higher paid professional employees rather than hourly workers, who, as I said, face a different set of issues, I think the key issues are programs that allow people to trade income for time, and that allow them to choose their schedules at the cost (and I think for these workers there is to some extent a trade-off that has to be made) of taking reduced current income or forgoing raises. The kinds of things I think we need to be seriously considering are job sharing, permanent upgraded part-time work, sabbaticals, vacation periods, and a shorter-than-12-month work year (e.g., administrative staff in a university can go on to academic schedules, that is, 9- or 10-month schedules with the loss of pay. At the University of Massachusetts they're giving workers the option to do this now in response to budget cuts.) I think we need to try voluntary programs first, giving government encouragement for them, but employers can begin to do this on their own. That will do two things. First, not everybody wants shorter schedules, so I don't believe that the solution for these kinds of workers is just to impose shorter hours. I think we need to set up options for people and have government and employers cooperate in making those really feasible options, reducing the penalties that are currently associated with shorter hours. The mechanics are fairly simple: time can be another element of the benefit package. People can select different working schedules, and the companies can cost those schedules out.

In the costing out, though, I should say that employers need to be sensitive to the fact that people will do more work in a shorter period of time. We don't want to penalize people: if their productivity is going up, they should be compensated for it (and we have to understand the connection there). We need to think in terms of time banks. Companies could establish time banks that could operate either on an annual basis or for a longer term in which people are allowed to save up time they can then take later, borrowing, lending, or spending time. But we have to begin to think about hours of work as something fungible that should be an integral part of every benefit package that is available to employees. There are real life-cycle issues here. People may want to work longer hours before they have children, or take shorter hours when they have children or are older. There are many dimensions to this.

Finally, on the legal side, we desperately need an amendment to the Fair Labor Standards Act to deal with salaried workers. I don't think a standard 40-hour week is feasible at this point so what I suggest is that we require every employer in this country to set a standard of hours for salaried jobs. Employers would have the flexibility to set any standard they want, 100, 80, 60, whatever it is. But we should force that declaration. When a person is hired or promoted into a job, there is a standard number of hours they are expected to work. If they work more hours, they will be compensated—paid hours will be put into their time bank. If there's a big project coming up and an employee is required to work 70-hour weeks for a couple of months and standard hours are 55, that worker will bank those extra 15 hours a week and can take a sabbatical, or an extra Friday or six months off. Right now, salaried workers have no protection with respect to working hours. They have no negotiation, and there is no standard. This is a real gap in the way we deal with salaried workers.

Finally, let me say one thing about the feasibility and popularity of these ideas. I've deliberately talked today about options that I do not believe are costly. Trading income for time is something that can be done on a cost neutral basis for organizations. Today, if we're thinking about practical implementation of new worktime schedules, that's an important thing because many companies are working under serious cost constraints. There are also cost savings associated with lower turnover, higher retention rates, better possibilities for recruitment, less absenteeism, all of which come out of programs that give people more control over the amount of time that they work.

The one problematic area at the moment is the way employers pay fringe benefits, because they're paid on a per-person basis. It's also part of why employers prefer long hours, because they don't want to hire more workers and entitle them to benefits. We need to change the benefits structure so people who work longer hours are more costly for the firm. I would like to see a move to the prorating of benefits. Actually, I would like to see medical benefits put into the public sphere altogether, but in the absence of that, if employers continue to pay health insurance (which I think is a terrible idea), then at least let's remove the perverse disincentive for short hours that has arisen with this system, which is that because employers pay these benefits and because they're paid per employee, employers want fewer people and they want them working longer hours. So let's prorate benefits to make it feasible for employees to work short hours, and make it more costly for employers to have workers working very long hours.

Finally, is this something that people want? The polls are increasingly showing desires for more time and even willingness to sacrifice current income for time. A very interesting poll asked people, "Would you like an extra day off a week, even at the loss of that day's pay?" A considerable majority of American workers now say they would like that option. That's not something that's yet available to them, but the time has really come now for some action on this. For the people we've been talking about today, the potential popularity of these programs is very great.

DISCUSSION

Q: I worked for a medium-sized law firm where, over about a three-year period, the associates unanimously voted that they did not want raises because they did not want their hours to go up. For all three of those years, they had raises and increased hours imposed on them. I now work for the State of California and for the last 18 months we had a 5 percent pay cut imposed on us and were given a day off per month to bank. Most people are not taking that time off because there's the potential that we will be repaid for that time; it will be essentially bought back from us by the state. It was very interesting to me because in the first situation people wanted less time and were willing to take less pay, but that was a choice they were making. With the state, it was not a choice, but something imposed on us, and people were not receptive. I was just curious if there are any data on the issue of voluntariness in terms of how people react.

JULIET SCHOR: I didn't really have time to get to the complexities of people's preferences about trading income for time, but I argued that there is growing interest in trading income for time, and I believe that there is. One of the things that's very clear over a long period of time, and this may be part of what you're seeing, is that there is much, much less willingness to cut current income than to give up future increases. Part of the reason is that people get locked into particular spending patterns, either because they're in debt and they have payments to make, or because they become used to a particular level. So cutting back, especially involuntarily, is and has always been an unpopular thing. I think that's part of why you're not seeing more receptivity to this.

On the other hand, there are interesting cases—these are of hourly workers, so they may not fit the situation you're talking about—where there were involuntary reductions in overtime, especially people being cut back to shorter schedules. Many of these hours were very long—55 to 60 hours a week—and these high overtime manufacturing workers were very unhappy about being cut back. But what cases like this have shown is that employees' lives changed a tremendous amount when they went from 60-hour-a-week jobs to 40-hour-a-week jobs. The quality of their lives increased so much that when the companies wanted to go back to the old ways, the workers said, "forget it," and they refused to volunteer for overtime anymore. I think the one day a month cut may be part of the issue too, and that one day a week would be much more attractive to people, because it allows them to change the structure of their lives in a more appealing way.

As far as the associates in the firm go, there's a new survey of Boston firms that sounds very similar, that is, a strong desire to trade income for time, and no ability to do so. This is another example of the ways in which the market is not providing people with the schedules they want.

I do believe the way a program of trading income for time is implemented is very important, and that the way to do it successfully is to give people the opportunity to trade for both current and future income, and to give them choice about how they will use the time, because there's a lot of diversity in people's preferences about the kinds of reduced worktime they want. We now have a very diverse society in terms of family structure and personal situation. People are going to be trying to work out all kinds of issues related to their spouse's work schedule, their children, or other demands on their time. The program should let people choose how the worktime reduction will occur. So maybe the problem in your example was also that the state was telling them, "This is when you will have the time." People should also have the ability to forgo raises rather than just have their current incomes cut. The fact that they had no say may have been part of the problem.

Q: How can your suggestions be implemented at the organizational level? How can we change the attitudes that have kept these outmoded structures in place?

JULIET SCHOR: This is a hard question, an age-old debate. As an economist, I have a tendency to think first about structure, particularly about incentives. So what I would like to see is a lot more thinking about ways in which incentives can change so that the incentives lead the employers to change the corporate culture or the institutional/organizational culture. That's why changes in the benefit structure, for example, or even putting in these kinds of programs that are advantageous to the employer, are good.

Here's another example of one that worked very well: United Airlines started a program called "Without Pay" among its reservation clerks. When the recession came it found it had more reservation clerks than it needed. These are very fungible people—they answer phones. They had too many people for the number of calls that were coming in. People were allowed to go up to the supervisors at any time and say, "I'd like to leave now," or "I'm not coming in tomorrow, I'll be gone for a week," or whatever it was, with the loss of that pay. It was a very popular program—something like 25 percent of total worktime was reduced because of people voluntarily taking time off. It was very much in the employer's interest as well, because they had been paying people they didn't need.

So, I think both are really important, there's no question about that. I don't think we can change the attitudes unless we have some underlying changes in the incentive structures. Unless the institutions see a reason to be behind this, they won't be. I think some of the personnel issues that are coming up may facilitate this; for example, difficulties retaining people because of work/family conflicts are becoming more serious, particularly among women. On the other side, of course, we have a growing pool of unemployed white-collar workers. That militates in the other direction and makes it easier for employers to see people as throwaway employees and not worry about losing them, because they know there's a very deep employee pool. I would be less than honest if I said that's not a serious issue right now. However, I have to come to this with a certain amount of optimism and believe that it's really a time in which it is possible to do something. I think it is, but I don't want to minimize the kinds of forces working in the other direction. I projected my trends in working time over the next 20 years and assumed the next 20 years look like the last 20 years. If current trends continue, we're looking at a 60-hour average work week in this country. So, I believe it's time to begin organizing about this. And of course, it's only through organization and collective action that institutions will change on this dimension. For people in professional and managerial kinds of jobs where unions don't exist as a possible vehicle for this, getting together to start an informal group to talk about worktime issues is the first step. Then go in a cooperative manner to higher management and say, "These are the kinds of programs we're thinking about. This is what people would like. These are the ways we think it can work."

Q: As you've said, it's a hard question. I was curious whether there have been any studies done in the private sector that might follow an organization that had the kinds of structures you describe, where the top management took advantage of that structure, and whether there were some differences when there was executive leadership setting a kind of example or model, if you will.

JULIET SCHOR: Not that I know of, although there is one student working at the Kennedy School at Harvard who's looking exactly at that question—the extent to which senior management leadership is important to change. It's not exactly on this issue, but I think it bears on it.

I should just mention that there is a paucity of examples of companies making serious changes in worktime structures. I know most people out here don't read the *New York Times*, but about 10 days ago a front page article on Europe going to the four-day work week appeared. And, as is always the case after something like this, scores of reporters across the country start working on stories on the four-day work week. And many of them called me. What was very interesting about this is that neither I nor they have been able to come up with examples of companies currently working four-day work weeks, except those who are working 40-hour weeks in 10-hour days, which out here is not unusual. We are working in uncharted territory. There are some companies doing some interesting things, but as far as radical changes in worktime, we don't have very many around at the moment, and those who do it are going to be real pioneers.

Q: I have a question about the implication of suggesting trading work for pay. It seems, again, the worker is asked to make the concession. One of the salient points I heard you make was about how productivity actually increases when you work less time. Couldn't we ask the employers to look more carefully and prove to them that, indeed, if workers are working less time, they actually might be more productive? It seems like employers are not forced to ask that question, or re-evaluate their attitude toward productivity. When hours are reduced, the worker is again asked to take less pay.

JULIET SCHOR: Yes, I think that's quite reasonable. Especially in situations where you have measured output. For example, one could very easily design schemes that give people shorter hours and then, after the first period of time (say, the first six months or year of this), adjust the pay based on what actually happened to productivity. Other kinds of savings are also reasonable. I've been having some preliminary discussions with a manufacturer who's interested in going to a six-hour day without a cut in pay, which is quite good. They believe they'll be able to make up the difference in a higher intensity of work and shorter breaks during the day (that is, cutting the lunch break and other breaks). For any of you who are involved in 24-hour operations and have a maintenance shift, you can reduce your maintenance shift to a six-hour rather than an eight-hour shift.

There's another dimension to this that is relevant to the four-day week, and we are going to be hearing a lot about this in coming weeks. Studies have been done with hourly workers, but I think it's also true with salaried workers, showing that cutting back small amounts of time—cutbacks to, say, a 35-hour work week, for example—typically involve no reduction in production and actually are of no cost to the employer, even when the pay rate stays the same, because the productivity is maintained. Going to a 35-hour work week with no cut in pay is basically something that is free to the employer. But it's very hard to get them to believe that up front. Even if we went to programs that said, "Let's do it on a trial basis for six months and then we'll talk about adjusting the compensation," I think that would be a step forward.

Q: You mentioned the notion of consumption interrelating with all these issues because if we reduce time, remain productive, and make more resources available for unemployment, then we have to do something else—like reduce consumption. Any ideas on that?

JULIET SCHOR: Yes. I talked at the beginning about the rise in productivity and the failure of hours to decline—in fact, about a substantial rise in working hours. I believe that this country got trapped into what I call a work-and-spend cycle, which means that we worked long hours, had high productivity growth, and used all that productivity growth to increase our material standard of living, kept our hours long, and so on. We have been caught, particularly people of middle- and upper-middle-class status—that is, people who are basically not in financial or material need, in a cycle of rising expectations. The standard of living we had in 1940 now seems to us very inadequate, and even the one we had in

1960, 1970, and probably 1980 seems so. As we move up the ladder, we look back and think that all these things that were once luxuries and yielded big increases in satisfaction have become just part of the landscape. We take them for granted now and so are always looking for the next increase.

The fundamental mindset in our country is one of improving our material standard of living, and if that's not happening, we think there's something very, very wrong. I've been talking about time and the quality of life because I think we've been sacrificing our quality of life with respect to time and in a way that is no longer working for people, no longer improving our quality of life. I think this is at the core of why people think that life is getting worse and society is in decline and the economy is in such bad shape, and why we feel things are falling apart around us. We've lost control over our time, and I do believe that we've got to think about reduced worktime in terms of trading off future increases.

I believe we should avoid getting trapped into the next cycle of accelerated consumption. I'm against high definition TV, for example. People in Washington think this is the answer to the country's competitiveness problem—we'll get it before the Japanese do, and isn't that a great thing? I just keep thinking about the fact that we keep going on to an increasingly sophisticated problem while we're perfectly happy with the way our television sets look today. Now we're going to have to work more hours to get high definition TV and we'll think it's great at first, but six months down the line we're going to forget about how much better it looks, we're not going to be able to look at our old color TVs because they'll look lousy, and we're not, in the end, going to have a more satisfying, meaningful, better, higher quality of life.

The poor and lower income groups are just as much trapped in this cycle. They're not making the income to have the goods, but they want them just as much. The culture of consumerism pervades every level of this society: the people who have the stuff and the people who don't, or the people who are trying to steal it from the ones who have it because they don't have it.

There's a lot that is positive about material goods and the increases in material standards of living, and I'm not saying we should go back to the way things were in the 1920s, when people didn't have washing machines and indoor plumbing. The question is, by 1990 or 2000, have we done enough to give ourselves a reasonable standard of living—after all, we have the highest standard of living the world has ever seen—and can we think about giving to ourselves in other ways and getting off what I see as a consumerist treadmill? Can we equalize more in society? In this country we have dealt with the inequalities of income by saying, "A rising tide lifts all boats." Let's have growth to give the poor and the people at the top more at the same time. Our current situation is now environmentally impossible, and in terms of what it's doing to our culture and the commercialization of culture, very pernicious.

Public Life vs. Private Life

Is there a Golden Mean?

GARY K. HART

It's a delight to be with you today. I was asked by Judith to give more of a personal dimension to some strategies for balancing the public and private that someone in a high profile position like mine has to utilize. My basic message is that there's got to be a balance. Generally speaking, people who in public life who don't have their private life together are not going to be great public servants.

I used to be a classroom teacher. In fact, last year I went back to the classroom and taught in an urban high school for a semester every day for four and one-half months to try and relive that experience, and maybe also to figure out whether I wanted to do that again when I complete my senatorial term. It was an interesting reality check: you forget that public school teachers don't have secretaries, don't have phones, work in a lot of obscurity and, as Aretha Franklin says, don't get a lot of respect. In the legislature we've got a lot of secretaries, way too many phones, and we don't operate in obscurity—that's for sure.

I have been in the legislature for 20 years—8 in the assembly, almost 12 now in the state senate. My district has 800,000 constituents, and over 100 miles of coastline. It used to include Malibu and parts of the San Fernando Valley, but under reapportionment, I now start in Ojai and Ventura and go up to the Monterey County line. It's a very big area—three counties, over 20 cities, and over 50 school districts, all of whom feel that I am their link to that bureaucracy in Sacramento. When the legislature is in session I get over 100 letters a day that need to be responded to promptly. We get many more phone calls from constituents, to say nothing about all the non-constituent calls. On any given day I probably get at least a dozen press calls that I feel somewhat obligated to return. Voters and constituents have very high expectations, which is appropriate in a democracy when you are a public servant. They expect me to be responsive. When they have a problem, they think that I can solve it, and they insist that I do my very best to accomplish that.

One aspect of my job that differs from most, of course, is that I have two places of work. I work in Sacramento, and I also work in Santa Barbara, which presents some special problems in terms of family. It's also a very public job in which anything you say or do is likely to appear the next day in the newspapers if you are not careful—and oftentimes even when you are careful.

With those parameters in mind, what I feel is so vital to this public-private balance is time. My wife is a part-time physician for Kaiser. One of the things that makes working for an HMO so attractive is that there is some predictability. You are not on call all of the time. The traditional small-town rural physician is on call all of the time. My wife is on call one weekend a month, one day out of the week, and when she is on call she works very hard, but the rest of the time she has some certainty that she can be home with the family.

In some respects, my job is like that of the small-town physician. I'm on call all the time. Yesterday there was a horrible shooting tragedy in Oxnard, which is part of my district, and most of yesterday was spent trying to deal with that tragedy. The day before, we had the conviction of two people in Sacramento on felony corruption charges—Paul Carpenter and Clay Jackson—both people I know, and lots of contact from the media wanting to know my views about them and what could be done to avoid these kinds of problems in the future. Last week I had a school district that was about ready to go under financially, unable to make payroll. I had to intervene. It was a crisis situation. Last month we had the fires here in Los Angeles. That always involves legislators. So there are crises in this job, and you're on call all the time. My secretary has been with me, thank goodness, for 20 years. She always knows where I am. She always has a way to get to me, which I sometimes resent. If you've been in that sort of situation for 20 years, the idea that there is going to come a time when no one has the right to know where you are is very liberating.

Last week I clipped an article from the *Los Angeles Times* where after the passage of NAFTA, the President's chief lobbyist in Congress announced that he was resigning after that great legislative success. He was quoted as follows:

> It isn't a question of hours. I knew that the job would have long hours. [But] the job doesn't end when one leaves the building. There are no recesses or weekends. The beeper and the phone do not respect any private time. And maybe I should have, after being an old man in this city, appreciated all of that, but I have a feeling that we have set new standards of intensity.

The article goes on to say that in the Clinton Administration there is some pride in the fact that the schedule for most staffers begins almost at dawn. People hardly leave before 9 p.m., and a lot of people are there until midnight. Until President Clinton took his well publicized Martha's Vineyard vacation, hardly any staffer had had a day off since he had assumed office. I think for us in the legislature it's difficult. And my impression is that for the executive offices of the governor's office and the presidency, the time pressures are even greater. One of the things that I have seen, having been in the legislature now for 20 years, is that you figure out ways to establish a system so that you are able to maintain your sanity. What is always difficult in elected positions is the first year or 18 months of trying to get established. In our form of government, where you have a new administration that normally comes in every four years, people are always working very hard to get up to speed.

One of the things that term limits is going to mean is that a lot more people will be elected for shorter periods of time. When people are in these positions, they are not going to have the luxury that I've had of being able to work out a system over a number of years. There are going to be even greater pressures upon legislators, who are going to be working in many instances at a very frenetic pace.

Let me talk about the strategies I've devised to work out a balance. As I mentioned, I work in two places—Santa Barbara and Sacramento—and am almost unique among Southern California legislators in that my family resides in Sacramento. The conventional political wisdom is that if you want to stay in office, your family has to reside in your district—that if you move to Sacramento, that's symbolic that you don't care about your constituents and that you're not linked to the community. The majority of any legislator's time is spent in Sacramento and not in their district, and so my wife and I decided that from a family standpoint, where I was spending the most time was where the family ought to be located. We took a deep breath and made the choice, thinking maybe this will be a major political liability, but it really hasn't turned out that way. And even though the time is almost balanced between Sacramento and the district, what happens for legislators who don't have their families in Sacramento is that when they go to Sacramento, after normal work hours they're alone. It's almost like a college experience all over again, and just like in college, people can get carried away.

When they return to the district, they say, well, that's going to be family time, but then Friday and Saturday are prime days for politicians; there are always dinners, and there are always parties that are command performances, so it's really the worst of both worlds. When they're in Sacramento they're alone and when they're back home they're not with their family. And so our family has made a different choice, and it's been a very healthy one for us, to live in Sacramento.

I once ran in a very competitive race against another assemblyman, Charles Imbrecht, when I moved from the assembly to the senate. I represented Santa Barbara County. He represented Ventura County. It was a marginal district and a very close race. In one of our first debates he said that for the four years that he had served in the state assembly, he had never spent a weekend outside of the district, that he was always on call in his district, and that if he was elected to the state senate, he would always be on call. And he said very gently, "I don't think that Hart can make a similar comment or pledge." I took it for what it was and said to the audience that he was absolutely right. If you want someone to be on call every day, no matter what, you really ought to vote for him. But I have a family, and they are important, as important if not more important than my constituents, and they come first on many days. And so if that's an important consideration for you, I urge you to vote for Imbrecht. He did not raise the issue again in the campaign.

I have also found that when you are in session in Sacramento, it seems as though every association has a convention there at some time during the year. The lawyers. The teachers. The dietitians. The used car salesmen. There is sort of a game that's played where these constituents show their clout with their legislator by getting their legislator to come to a cocktail party or go out to dinner. If legislators decline, it's not received well by some constituents, particularly if they are the only ones who can't deliver. But I've used the same strategy with my constituents as I've used with Imbrecht, which is that I'd love to come, but if I go to all these events I'll never be able to see my family. And people do back off, at least in their dealings with me—I don't know what they say privately. What I say is, rather than me come to a cocktail party and be there for 45 minutes and have a hard time hearing what anyone says, drop by the office and we'll have 10 minutes of whatever you want to share with me in terms of legislation. It's been a reasonable trade-off, and I think it's worked very well.

We also have a rule in our family that I'm entitled to one night a week out, because there are certain times when you have to be out. But that's the rule that operates in our family. Dinner is served every night at 7:00, and I drop what I'm doing almost without exception in order to be there at least four nights out of five during the week, because it's a priority, and I don't think it has really affected my ability to be a good legislator.

One of the things that's happened this year in the legislature is a change in policy regarding starting time. Before, you'd call a committee meeting for 9:30, or a floor session for 9:30, and you'd be lucky if it started at 10:00; normally, it'd start at 10:30. It was ridiculous. Time is valuable, and you'd come and sit around and wait. It was sort of a joke because the freshman legislators would come and sit around and look sort of foolish. In the culture of legislators it's an unstated assumption that the more important you are, the later you are for meetings. It is very important to not be there until business has actually begun. For those of us that want to be home with our families or somewhere else besides spending 18 hours a day in the legislative arena, it was terribly inefficient. To their credit, the new freshman class that came in—there were substantial numbers of them—made as their highest legislative priority this year that we are going to start on time. And now in the state assembly, they have a process whereby if the session is at 8:00, you have to be present at 8:15. If you are not present by 8:15, you have to stand up and state your reasons for being late. It's like school. And it's working.

I also wanted to mention that because long hours are involved in my job, one of the things I try to do is make special accommodations for my children. We have three daughters, all of whom are school age, and because of the nature of my position, there are opportunities that I think are wonderful for children. So I've tried to involve my kids in my work. Two of my daughters, who are in high school, have worked the summer as receptionists in the office. They've had an opportunity to see what my life's work is like by just answering the phones. It's a very revealing experience for anyone—including daughters.

We have also found over the years that one of the things we do both in campaigns and at the holidays is put out a lot of mail. And young children, at least in our household, are fascinated to lick envelopes, believe it or not. It's one of the most dreadful chores in politics, but kids really enjoy doing it, and we built upon that. We have a family photo that goes in the cards, and now they are involved in designing the cards. It's sort of their project. It's not only for my constituents, but it's also for their friends. And that's worked very well.

We also try at least once a week, and I don't try to structure this too much, to have a talk about what's going on in terms of politics and my life at the State Capitol. On occasion, it's led to some interesting legislation. For example, my daughters are tall, and tall helps, obviously, if you play volleyball or basketball. So they're involved in competitive sports, and they're also good students. They complained about the fact that they have to take P.E. (as required by law) in addition to volleyball, and thus spend as much time doing sports as they do academics. So we introduced a bill to try and change that, and my daughter testified. We also had a discussion after the Clarence Thomas-Anita Hill situation about sexual harassment where I asked my daughters whether or not they thought sexual harassment was a problem at school. They looked at me like I was crazy. "Are you kidding? Of course it's a problem." And I had never heard this before. They said inappropriate touching and offensive comments are big problems. And so we went to work and ended up introducing a bill on sexual harassment in the schools that was enacted last year and has been quite a media issue. *CBS News* ended up calling, and my daughter was interviewed on *CBS Evening News with Dan Rather.* So we've had an opportunity to do some things in that domain that I think have helped bridge the distance between family and work that have been very nice.

I also wanted to say a little bit about spousal relationships. It seems to me that there are three different arrangements that I have seen in the Capitol. The first, and we're talking primarily about male legislators and female spouses, is the sort of traditional arrangement where the male legislator works and the wife is responsible primarily as a homemaker. When I was first elected to the legislature that was a fairly common arrangement. It is much less so today, as it is for society as a whole. But at first glance, I thought that would probably be the most functional arrangement: one person working very busily and the other sort of there as support. In fact, it was the least satisfactory arrangement I saw. There were more tensions and difficulties—and, I think, divorces—as a result of those kinds of relationships. The problem was that there were so many interruptions in the legislators' lives, particularly if they didn't think it through and manage it properly, that it became very frustrating and caused a lot of resentment, particularly for the at-home spouse.

The second kind of arrangement for the spouse is a kind of political partner who helps in the operation. You might think of Hillary Rodham Clinton, who has been such a star, as the par excellence model of this approach. The kind of political arrangement I see in Sacramento in marriages is not one of equality; the female spouse tends to be the junior partner, works in the office, and functions as sort of support staff to the operation. Between husband and wife that seems to work very well. But I've seen many instances where for the rest of the staff, it's cause for some resentment, because the rules don't quite apply to the spouse as they do to the other people in the office. And in many instances, it seems it would be better if that arrangement didn't exist, at least as far as those other staff members are concerned.

Last, there's the arrangement that I have, and that I feel most comfortable with, and that is to have an equal professional spouse who has a professional life of her own and who is not actively involved in my career. She is part of the Christmas photo and some other things but basically has a life of her own. All of the questions about quality time and how to deal with children enter in, but with a part-time job for my spouse it's worked very well for us.

Nevertheless, one area I find particularly difficult, and the reason I'm getting out of politics, is campaigning. In campaigning, everything is intensified. These days if you want to run for legislative or statewide office in California you have to give two years of your life to the process. I did this in 1988 when I ran for Congress and barely lost. It was a very competitive race, and I was on the go 18 hours a day for at least six days a week. All of those nice rules I told you about that our family has devised went out the window during this one year of campaigning. As a result, there was a year where I just didn't know anything about my kids. Their development during that period went almost completely unnoticed. It was very frustrating.

I began this year wanting to run for the state constitutional office of superintendent of public instruction. It was a two-year commitment to go out and raise a jillion dollars, requiring 18-hour days. But after about three months, my heart just wasn't in it. My oldest daughter at the time was 16, and I realized that by the time I finished the campaign, she would be off to college and away from home. Basically it would be the end of our relationship in the traditional father-daughter sense, and I just didn't feel right about that. It wasn't where I wanted to be. So I bailed out.

I think this problem is particularly difficult in presidential campaigns. I see that the Republican candidates have already been in New Hampshire for the last three or four months. It used to be that you began a presidential campaign about 18 months before the election. But Jack Kemp and all those people have been in New Hampshire and Iowa since August 1993—four years before the next election. Running for statewide office for two years is difficult, but when you run for president for three or four years, in terms of family relationships it's ridiculous.

I might also suggest that what's happening with the elongation of these campaigns, particularly for president, is that this process really is a leg up for people who don't have anything else to do except campaign. Thus we have a whole series of presidential candidates from Jesse Jackson, Ross Perot, and Ronald Reagan, who were unemployed, basically, to vice-presidents, who many people feel are unemployed. You have a whole series of people who run for president because they're about the only people who can withstand the all-consuming process. That's not a very healthy system.

I think we're also running the risk of having people in high positions who don't have children or family responsibilities. Now, Clinton and Gore are exceptions to that, but it's a trend that I think is somewhat troublesome. There is also a trend that personal wealth counts for a lot more. Time has become so important because our campaigns, now, are so media-based, and the way you get media is to buy time. Time is money. If you have personal wealth, you are able to buy it and other people have to scramble: it really gives a leg up to people who are wealthy.

What can be done about all this in terms of structural change? Conventional answers include public financing of campaigns so we get away from the heavy emphasis upon money and everybody has the same amount of money—that is an important variable that impacts upon time, and shorter campaigns. The British have a great system. They take six weeks and it's sort of a surprise call by the prime minister. We need to figure out a way to shorten our process. One law passed by California voters, thrown out by the courts, and put before the courts again involves placing a restriction or prohibition in off-year fundraising so you can only raise money for an office during a 12-month cycle. That might be a step in the right direction, although I'm sure there'll be some very entrepreneurial ways that people will find to get around such a thing.

I wish we could reinvigorate parties. The Mayor Dalys of the world got a critical rap back in the 1960s, so we made a lot of changes in our system. But if we had a stronger party system, where candidates were not so frenetic to reach the voters personally, I think that would help.

On a bolder, more creative note, more women are going to be elected to public office. And just as I've seen with my wife, who wanted to have children and be a professional, who endured residency and children simultaneously, and who worked very hard to secure part-time arrangements, more and more women are going into medicine and forging change in residency programs. My hope is that as more women serve in the public arena, change will occur largely because of the demands of people in the profession.

Let me throw out a couple of off-the-wall ideas. We talk a lot about job share. No one has ever talked about job-sharing for legislators. If there was ever a job that two people or many people ought to be able to handle, it would be a job as a state senator. A job share for the state senate position could do a great deal to educate people about the possibilities of job-sharing. I'm not even sure whether it's constitutional: what do you do when two individuals don't agree on a vote?

An even crazier idea involves giving some serious consideration to having as part of our legislative body people who are not elected—people who are appointed to legislative positions. Because of the nature of campaigning, people who run for office are too often just fund raisers and public relations types. They are not scientists, they are not successful business people, they are not artists, they are not academics—part of the mix of what you want in a legislative body. In the British system, again, they have a House of Lords. I wouldn't want to carry that analogy too far, but there is an appointment process. They don't have the full responsibility that members of the House of Commons have. But having some way that ordinary people could participate in the legislative arena who come out of a different line of work would have a salutary effect on our legislative bodies.

I think it was Freud who said to be healthy you've got to do two things: you've got to be able to love and work successfully. What I've seen in politics is that people work very hard; the love aspect, if we can talk about that in terms of your personal life and relationships, is where it gets all screwed up. The work takes so much that there is not any time for love. But in a sense there is always time for love. It just takes neurotic forms. In politics there is a lot of egotism and pursuit of fame that becomes sort of a form of love. If you don't have a personal life, the temptations and seductions of fame and publicity take over and drive every part of the decision-making process.

Where you stand depends on where you sit. We determine our priorities and make our basic decisions based on our life experiences and what we do on a day-to-day basis. One of the things that I find very frustrating is that every politician talks about the importance of family and the importance of children. And yet their own families and their own children oftentimes do not get the time of day. We see the decline of support for children's programs, services, and budgets, and it's a function, in part, of the fact that our politicians don't have time for their own children, their own families. If legislators can't be sensitive to their own children, how can we expect them to be sensitive to poor children in faraway places? Legislators who have been able to figure out some way to balance the public and the private, the love and the work, are those that are the most effective politicians and the people that I feel most comfortable working with.

DISCUSSION

Q: It seems to be the rare person in politics who strives for the balance between their work and their personal life, and you're leaving politics.

GARY HART: I am leaving elective politics after being in the business for 25 years. I feel that I've paid my dues.

Q: You're not excused.

GARY HART: It doesn't mean that you can't do it. It's just that, for me, I'm selfish enough to want to do something a little bit different after 25 years. I've seen so many people in Sacramento who have overstayed their welcome, and I don't want to be in that category. Certainly you and I know that elected officials work full time. But still they take time away from the demands of the workplace, the constituency, the legislative job, and make certain that some of it goes to the family. You've done that and I take great pride in the fact that I always did that as well. But I want to point out that, for the most part, you don't get credit for having balance in your life at all.

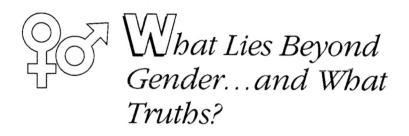

What Lies Beyond Gender...and What Truths?

EMILY LEVINE

Introduction by Helen S. Astin

In *The New York City Stick Ball Team Improvisational Comedy Group* Emily was always cast as the girl. And she was, in fact, the only girl in the group. From the only girl, she became the only person on the stage in a one-woman show, *Myself, Myself, I'll Do It Myself,* which she wrote and performed herself. This led her to the world of stand-up comedy. Emily has written and performed an Emmy Award-winning series of commercials, she has written two screenplays, *Fast and Furious* and *Snatched,* and she has acted in both L.A. and New York. The *Village Voice* claims that she is a brilliant comedienne.

In December 1989, Emily took some time off to read philosophy, feminist theory, chaos theory, and quantum physics. From this research, she created a new work in progress, *Chaos, Paradox, Ballroom Dancing.* Emily went back to television in 1991 when she signed on as a producer of the first season of *Room for Two* and became the new head writer on *Designing Women.* I have had the pleasure of listening to Emily, learning from her while at the same time I laughed. And it's wonderful to combine scholarship, hard thinking, activism, and humor. We are indeed in for a treat.

Emily, I see her as a special friend. A funny person. A very creative and perceptive woman. A supporter of our cause and work. I had the pleasure, also, and I'll share that with the group, of spending some time with Emily, both of us trying to learn how to meditate. We all need that part in our lives. We were not very good students, but we had a wonderful time together. I welcome Emily and I present you, Emily Levine.

EMILY LEVINE: Thanks. I appreciate that introduction, although none of it would explain my presumption in describing myself as a philosopher. The reason for that derives from a transition I began making three years ago when I realized I wasn't going to go very far as the "Spinoza of Comedy" and thought I might try being instead the "Lou Costello of Philosophy." Instead of asking who's on first, I would ask why. So what follows is a sometimes unwieldy mix of ideas and jokes and I invite you to help me grapple for balance by asking for more jokes or more ideas as you see fit.

Were you, of course, to actually do so, you would be breaking the boundary between performer and audience, which is precisely what I'm interested in doing. In fact, boundaries in general are what I've been thinking about lately in my philosopher mode. It seems that every issue with which we are confronted nowadays can be construed as a boundary issue, from the war in Bosnia to the rapes of the women in Bosnia—which is a double boundary issue: the violation of a personal boundary that constitutes rape and then the exclusion of the rape victim from the community. From the ringing of cellular phones at concerts—the line between private and public, to eating disorders like bulimia and anorexia—controlling what goes in and what goes out. There is an implicit boundary issue even in this item in the *National Enquirer* about a lion tamer who had been severely mauled by his lion: "Mr. Russell, who learned lion taming through a correspondence course..."—the line between sanity and insanity!

But particularly in line with the title of this conference, and in general as people begin to talk more and more of the "boundaryless corporation," I think it fruitful to examine how boundary issues operate in the workplace. First, I must admit that my experience in a normal workplace is limited because I did stand-up comedy for many years, during which time the closest I came to a corporation was the Mafia...which turned out to be very close indeed. In fact, I had lunch one day with a Mafia man and he gave me my first insight into corporations. He said that he would never hire a woman because, and I quote, "a woman doesn't know how to become your slave...Men, you know, will start working for you, then they'll borrow a little money from you, and before you know it, you own them." Women, on the other hand, he said disdainfully, "don't get it."

I didn't realize how extraordinarily accurate this was until I went to work in television. Again, I must add a disclaimer that television is a field somewhat removed from ordinary reality. For example, a studio executive once criticized my proposed story for a pilot episode of a series because he didn't think it was "real" enough, then told me a story he'd thought up. When I said, honestly, that I didn't understand why his story was "realer" than my story, he answered, "Because you've seen mine on television before."

So we're talking about a medium in which reality is understood to be self-referential. Again, to illustrate, when I finally agreed to an overall deal with the Walt Disney Company, after much resistance, my manager called to say they were so excited they were sending me a present. Then it was my turn to be excited—I thought I'd be getting a Baccarat vase, one of those corporate presents that, like a wedding present, you never use but take out occasionally to show where you've come in the world. Imagine my surprise when they sent a three-foot high stuffed Mickey Mouse. I knew immediately I'd made a terrible mistake. In agreeing to the deal, I'd effectively agreed to subordinate my own aesthetic and way of thinking to the company aesthetic, the company ethic. To add insult to injury, when I looked in the catalogue to see how much this gift had cost, the description of the three-foot high mouse was "life-sized."

So I think there is a very striking boundary issue that obtains in this particular workplace between fantasy and reality. In the fantasy world of television—"telereality," I call it—there is no institutionalized sexism and no institutionalized racism. While you may have an individual bigot, you cannot in any way show that the institutions themselves are sexist or racist or classist or any other "ist." But my argument, as has been made brilliantly by Joan

Acker and by other people, is that our institutions are already sex-ist in the very way we structure them—what lines we draw, where we draw them, who draws them, and, indeed, what we think a line is. I want to argue further that "sex" is male and female and there is a boundary between them and the name of that boundary is "gender." And whether that boundary is a fantasy or a reality is what I want to explore here in terms of how it affects these structures.

And now I'm very much afraid I have to explain the universe. Because how we think the universe is structured has a great deal to do with how we structure things. And maybe, again, it's just my experience from being in the film and television industry, but I do believe the universe is pretty much exactly like my life. One day you read in the paper that the universe, which we once thought to be made up of matter, is also made up of something called dark matter, which doesn't shine as matter does, which we don't see, or at least which we don't recognize, but which, scientists now think, accounts for 90 percent of the universe...the exact same percentage of the Screen Actors Guild who are never seen in anything, or at least anything that matters. And in an article about giant galactic structures which may actually be dark matter, the *L.A. Times* describes them as "gaseous, celestial bodies that failed to reach stardom." So as far as I'm concerned, Broadway, the Milky Way, it's the same thing.

Or take Pythagoras...please. Pythagoras was the first to say that the universe could be perfectly described by math. And, by happy chance, the universe that math described was perfect—or-derly, precise, rational, and therefore beautiful, with nice straight lines defining everything. So committed were he and his followers to this vision that when they discovered irrational numbers, twisted and irregular, and therefore ugly, they decided no one outside their sect was to hear of or know about them, thus prov-ing that there is nothing new under the sun, including the "don't ask, don't tell" policy. Furthermore, during a boat voyage com-prised almost entirely of Pythagoreans—a sort of Pythagorean Love Boat—they found in their midst the man who discovered the square root of two, the most irrational number in the universe, and threw him overboard. (And we complain about political correctness.)

So basically, to protect the beauty of their universe, their aesthetic, the Pythagoreans invented an ethic of denial. Anything "irregular" was thrown overboard. They denied that it existed, that it mattered. And while Pythagoreanism peaked around 500 B.C. it was in the summer of 1993 that Sandra Day O'Connor ruled against a voting district in South Carolina that had been gerrymandered to better represent the African-American vote because, she wrote, the line was "too twisted," it was "too irregular." Thus does the same prejudice operate and shape our institutions today.

The "scientific" values that both shape this Pythagorean-Newtonian-Sandra Day O'Connor universe and are reflected by it are rationality, objectivity, and linearity. Rationality suggests there is a clear line of thinking; objectivity suggests there is a viewpoint from which you can see the whole and therefore draw a straight line; and linearity implies that time is a line, that you start at the beginning and go step by step, in a cause and effect pattern, until you reach the end of the line, or your deadline, which is when you wish maybe time wasn't a line in the first place.

Now, these principles share an interesting characteristic, which is that each one has a line drawn through it to begin with. Rationality separates head and body, brain and heart, mind and matter. Objectivity separates subject and object. Linearity separates life and death. Yet another principle, reductionism, separates what matters and what doesn't matter. There is a reason for these divisions: the logic that underpins them—the logic of classical science and the Enlightenment—is dualism, and the whole business of dualism, or either/or thinking, is drawing a line, separating things in two. Furthermore, as the term either/or suggests, it's not just separating a phenomenon into two things, but two opposite things. So either people are rich or they're poor. Either they're black or they're white. Either I'm right or you're wrong. This is why I'm nervous about the opprobrium directed against women who "want it all." Because the opposite of "women who want it all" are women the way we like them, "women who want nothing."

And by the way, I'm not against dualism in itself. For one thing, that would be dualistic. For another, obviously, we all have an innate inclination towards dualism. We all have two eyes, two hands, two legs, and two voices in our heads—the voice that says, "Go ahead, take a risk" and the voice that says "Play it safe, think about your pension fund." The voice that says, "You can fix the clock on your VCR" and the voice that says, "No matter what you do it will say 12-12-12-12-12." (Some of us actually have more than two voices. I personally have 50 minimum. From the moment I wake up in the morning, it's "write a script," "clean the house," "read *A Brief History of Time*." Sometimes I envy Joan of Arc; all she ever heard was one voice—"Save France." Okay, it was a big thing to do but at least she could concentrate.)

And, also, I think dualism can be fair. Dualism was fair during the gas shortage in California in the late 1970s. They invented a dualistic solution. On odd days you could get gas, on even days you couldn't. Completely mathematical, completely fair. But then why don't they use it for everything? Why don't they use it for all those divisions that plague us, on which we can never seem to come to consensus? So on odd days you could have an abortion, on even days you couldn't. On odd days when a tree falls in the forest it does make a sound, on even days it doesn't. That way we could get on with our lives.

But I don't think dualism—as an ethic—is interested in fairness. Because once you have a spectrum defined as a straight line, and you've cut out everything in the middle so you only have two ends, people think they only have two choices. Right or wrong, good or bad, paper or plastic. Really, the extent to which people subscribe to this notion is amazing. Here's a letter to the *New York Times'* Art and Entertainment Section:

> To the Editor: I was disappointed that Mr. Ostreich did not cite WNCN's...most galling affront: (the) unscheduled and increasingly frequent insertions of New Age music...After a year or so of these, my family and I moved out of New York.

Listen to New Age music or move out of New York. Change the station? Not, apparently, an option.

So the problem is that when we visualize a spectrum as a horizontal line, then cut out the middle so the two ends are as far apart as possible, inevitably separate becomes apart-hate (apartheid). One thing becomes good and one thing becomes bad. Look at the 1992 Republican convention—it wasn't rich people and poor people, white people and black people, gay people and straight people; it was poor people and good people, black people and good people, gay people and good people. One side dominates the other. The horizontal line becomes vertical. That's why I always see that police helicopter flying over South Central Los Angeles as emblematic of this kind of dualism—white America looking at black America from as far away and up above as possible.

If, then, the line that we use to structure our society is a straight vertical line, the next question we must ask is, "Who draws the line?" In addressing this, I want to talk about three separations that become dominations—subject/object, private/public, and head/body—and how they're all connected.

Subject and object is most familiar to us from grammar. As anyone who ever had to parse a sentence will remember, the subject is the king of the sentence, the mover and shaker; the subject directs the action, the verb, to work upon the object. The subject is active, and the object is passive. The sentence is the grammatical equivalent of the missionary position. And if there's any doubt as to who's on top, one need only look at a book called *The Bonds of Love*, by Jessica Benjamin, in which she cites the observation by a psychoanalyst of signs in the newborn nursery of a hospital: over the little boys' cribs, the signs said, "I'm a boy"; over the little girls' cribs, the signs said, "It's a girl." Thus the little boy/subject is self-defining, while the little girl/object is only what the subject is not. So, if the I of the boy/subject is active, the you of the girl/object is passive. If I'm dominant, you must be submissive. If I'm independent, you must be co-dependent. Basically, it's I'm Chevy Chase and you're not.

I must insert here that although I thought my concept of explaining subject/object by comparing it with sentence structure was original, I have recently discovered better scholars than I have already thought of it and, worse, written about it. I found this out in the course of auditing a seminar at USC on "Sex and Gender in Ancient Greece and Rome," taught by Amy Richlin, no mean scholar herself. And that's not all I found out. As it turns out, the ancient Greeks and Romans had very specific definitions of active and passive as it relates to male and female and for them to reach this definition, there were two conditions necessary that I think have to be addressed.

As to the first of these conditions, they arrived at the definition of what it means to be masculine, to be an active male, in a homosexual environment, if one can use the term "homosexual" to mean "of the same sex" and not "lover of the same sex." The all-male environment in ancient Greece and Rome was itself a product of the distinction between private and public. The private sphere, the home, at least according to Hannah Arendt, was the arena of survival and procreation—all those things that relate to the body and to its sustenance, what she calls labor—and, therefore, prone to the violence of what we would now call natural selection; it was unsuited to democracy, according to the Greeks, but rather needed the strong hand of the despot/father to wield the competing points-of-view into one subjectivity. Having managed to do so, the head of the household could go forth into the public place and present his united family's subjectivity to other free men.

For a long time, until the second wave of the women's movement, in fact, our contemporary definitions of "masculinity" and the active "male" depended also on a strict division between private and public. Institutions of higher learning, the workplace, the armed forces, the football field—all these were the exclusive domain of men. It was no accident that football became the metaphor for the corporate ethic and at the same time the rationale by which women were excluded from top management positions in the corporation, accused of not knowing how the game is played. (Football also, not coincidentally, could stand for a metaphor of the separation of head and body that hierarchy requires. Football players are not supposed to think but to take orders from the quarterback, just as foot soldiers take their orders from headquarters, both in pursuit of the same end, pushing the line forward into the enemy's territory. Now, of course, both the football field and the front lines of combat remain the only places still holding the line against the incursion of women. I'll come back to this point.)

But in those arenas into which women were admitted, what we call the public sector, those men committed to a masculinist ideology retreated to the private sector. They began pushing to privatize government services; they took, and continue to take refuge in (white) male-only clubs like the Bohemian Grove where they can make public policy in private. These masculinist ideologues are both Republican and Democrat, conservative and liberal; it was, after all, ex-California Governor Pat Brown who recently defended the male-only policy of the Bohemian Grove by saying women should have their own place to do womanly things, like knitting and sewing, while men needed a place to do manly things, like pissing on redwood trees. I personally don't think these are comparable activities—sewing and knitting require figure-field perception, eye-hand coordination, fine motor dexterity, for one thing; more worrisome, one wonders what kind of great thinking comes out of an all-male enclave of this kind...possibly the trickle-down theory.

As for the second condition which necessitated the specific definitions of active and passive, if the context for the construct of masculinity in ancient Greece and Rome was homosexual in terms of being homogenous—all male—it was not all men as equals. Both Greece and Rome were slave societies. And what we today call "homosexuality," that is, sexual activity between members of the same sex, was endorsed, even encouraged, between freed men and slave boys. This was done without endangering the "masculinity" of the male because to be masculine meant to be the active subject which in turn meant specifically that you were the penetrator, regardless of the sex of the penetrated, passive, object. Indeed, so passive was the slave boy supposed to be that he was to betray no evidence of enjoyment, he was merely to suffer the act. (The Latin word for being penetrated, *patior*, also means to suffer, and is the word origin for that most classic of womanly virtues, patience.)

The connection between this definition and the workplace became clear to me when I read Petronius' Satyricon, in which a freed man (because there was upward mobility even in Rome; one could hope one day to buy one's freedom) reflects upon his youth as a slave thusly:

> ...for 14 years I was the old boy's fancy, and there's nothing wrong with it if the boss wants it, but I did all right by the old girl, too.

So while a slave man may suffer being penetrated, being passive, being an object, he at least has the compensation of being the subject, the penetrator, the active male vis-à-vis the boss' wife, or his own wife at home. Likewise, it seems to me, an important compensation in the contract between the CEO and the corporate drone, the modern "slave" in the Mafia man's parlance, is that while he agrees essentially to being "screwed" by his superiors—that is, being ordered about, being humiliated—he retains the privilege of "screwing" (in the more literal sense) women, thus retaining some claim to masculinity. Equally importantly, he has the added promise, and incentive, of moving up in the organization to eventually become the screwer, the master, the penetrator, the CEO himself. (To offer such a promise to a woman would be ludicrous since she can never be the penetrator in the literal sense so important to this construct.)

So at heart, it seems to me, the construct of masculinity in this society is based on a homosexual (homogenous), master/slave, sado-masochistic relationship. Indeed, not to belabor this, but I once read Anne Rice's pornographic oeuvre—it's politically correct because the slaves are men and women and the masters are men and women—and the definition of a good master proffered by the slaves was one who has no ambivalence about his mastery: he takes control and is completely dominant. Almost immediately afterwards, I read a pulp mystery novel by

Dick Francis in which the boss at the Jockey Club is praised as a good boss because he has no ambivalence about being a boss: he takes control, he's not afraid to be in total charge. So when I read recently about a town in California where the football team was cancelled due to lack of interest, and one boy said it was the coach's fault—"He didn't respect us," and the coach countered with the sincere lament—"They confuse disrespect with discipline," I thought, oh, no, they don't. Because "discipline" in the corporate world or on a football field is like the "discipline" of sado-masochism: it is designed to humiliate. And it's the separation of the head and body again because he who is made the body is so nervous about mastering himself that he projects the ability on to someone else. We pay an enormous price for feeling safe.

If, then, the construct of masculinity that dominates the workplace—the public place—derives from and is justified by the idea of the male as penetrator, it is clear that the promise offered the male "slave" to compensate for being "screwed" cannot be offered to a woman—she can never be a master, a CEO, since she lacks the vital equipment essential to that role. So, also, can we see that the sexual harassment to which women in the workplace are subjected is all about men proving that they're the penetrators. Their point is transgressing the line, whether it's the line between private and public, appropriate or inappropriate, or my body and your body. By transgressing that line, you're penetrating someone else's space. You're saying they don't have the materiality to occupy space. You're saying they don't matter.

Even men who think of themselves as liberal, who are in most respects liberal, find their (probably unconscious) ideological foundations threatened when women take their place as equals. A few years ago, Jimmy Breslin, in a celebrated incident, was challenged in a computer message by an Asian-American co-worker at the Daily News. He flew into a fury, confronting her in person, calling her a "slant-eyed yellow c***." (I find the use of that word significant, indicating as it does a place to be penetrated.) Unacknowledged was the idea that, welcome the presence of women in the workplace though he might, the fact that she had challenged him, had dared to think of herself as a subject, as someone whose point of view could help shape the public perception of "reality," was insupportable. He became completely bonkers.

Or look at the white judge who presided over the Winnie Mandela trial in South Africa. He sentenced her particularly harshly, he said, because, although found guilty, she was "unblushing." He expected to see on her black face the same evidence of shame he would see on his own white one. She didn't even exist for him other than as a projection of his own visage; she had no materiality.

And finally, to return to one of the last strongholds of masculinist ideologues, the armed forces—who serve, according to a writer in *z Magazine*, as the "border patrol" along the boundary of genders—if you look at their panic about gay people in the military, it's all about penetration. Are gay men passive or active? Will gay men rape the right people, i.e., women? And, okay, I know that sounds crazy, I know I went over the line on that one, but if you listen to people on the other side of the line, the officials who argue against women serving on the front lines, they're no less extreme. A Pentagon spokesman was quoted in the *New York Times* as saying that women shouldn't be allowed in combat because men are distractible. At the sight of a pretty woman, male soldiers might fire their rifles in the wrong direction or drive their tank into a ditch. A few months earlier, I heard a policeman on television offer similar reasons as to why women shouldn't be traffic cops—because male drivers are distractible and at the sight of a pretty woman will smash their car into the vehicle in front of them. Now, I don't want to spend a lot of time here discussing whether or not men are distractible. Let's say for the sake of argument they are. My question is, if they are so distractible that at the sight of a woman they will fire their rifles in the wrong direction or smash their cars into the one in front...why give them guns? Why put them in charge? Why let them draw the lines?

And now before this degenerates into a round of male-bashing, let me say a few words about essentialism, the idea that women have an essential female nature and men have an essential male nature. Not just Marilyn Quayle but many feminists sub-scribe to this essentialism, only taking back the right to define their essential natures themselves and, usually, defining them as superior to men's. Personally, as one who had trouble enough try-ing just to be a Superwoman, being a Goddess has no appeal. But beyond this, I have difficulty with the essentialist argument, even at its most seductive, as presented by Jung, for instance. (And let me say here, I am no psychoanalyst. I have read some Freud and, while many feminists express surprise at this, I think he is right about some things. I think, for instance, he is right about penis envy, I just think he is wrong about who has it.) Still, I offer my interpretation of Jung, who holds that the essential female nature, the anima, is connected to the unconscious. It doesn't actually do anything; it is merely a vessel through which the unconscious flows. The essential male nature, on the other hand, the animus, is completely action oriented; it does up the kazoo, but since it is cut off from the unconscious, without the intervening beneficence of the anima, its doing-ness may be either meaningless or, worse, destructive. One may say that we all hold within ourselves these male and female counterparts; certainly, I do. Many's the morning I have gotten into my car to go do an errand in Beverly Hills and I'm in the anima mode, the unconscious is flowing through me, and before I know it I'm halfway to Pasadena...at which point the animus kicks in and finds a reason to go to Pasadena, however stupid that reason may be. Whether these parts are truly "male" and "female," however, is open to question, and as long as a mas-culinist ideology is in place—an ideology that not only favors the conscious (rationality) over the unconscious (irrationality), but in-vented the top/bottom vertical line to begin with—I'm not sure that overturning the vertical line is as much of a solution as re-imaging the line.

And the clue for this new image derives directly from men like the Pentagon spokesman, like Jimmy Breslin, like the police-man—men who hold claim as men to being rational, but who in defense of their male prerogatives tip completely over into the ir-rational. This suggests to me that a line is not a continuum with two opposite ends, but a circle; the further you go to the extreme of your position, the closer you are to the extreme of your opposite. I call this the principle of transformation. I have no scientific proof of this, no formal logic to support it, nothing in fact but an old Donovan song which I am usually too embarrassed to cite — "First there is no mountain, then there is a mountain, then there is; caterpillar sheds his skin to show the butterfly within..."—still, I think we are headed in the direction of being able to reconfigure our viewpoint to encompass this principle.

I can say this, of course, because of dualism. People come out of the womb either as optimists—looking forward, saying "What brave new world is this?"—or pessimists, looking backward, saying, "What the hell was that?" So we have paranoids and delusionaries, and as one of the latter, I see a new worldview dawning. I can, however, lay claim to some reality basis for this hope because our physics is changing, which means the way we view the universe, our cosmology, is also changing. That's why everyone's so interested in cosmetology. When you don't know what the universe looks like, you start to worry about what you look like.

And I won't explain this shift in depth right now except to say that it involves quantum physics and chaos theory. These are sciences that expose the myth of "objectivity" and grapple with complexity instead of relying solely on reductionism. The universe they explore is irregular and irrational and non-linear. There are numerous new models offered by these scientists—fractals, Julia sets, etc.—for rethinking our ideas about what a line is or what a boundary is, but I want to focus on a new logic that was necessitated by the birth of quantum physics, when De Broglie resolved the long-fought debate about light. For years physicists had argued, some saying, "Light is a wave," some saying, "No, it's a particle." Then along came De Broglie like Faye Dunaway in *Chinatown* saying light is a wave and a particle.

This and-and logic, along with fuzzy logic, which still looks at a spectrum as a horizontal line but at least puts back the middle and celebrates ambivalence as well as bivalence, suggests a new ethic. Instead of denial, which allows one side to dominate—obliterate—the other, we have ambivalence, or paradox, which allows two apparently contradictory realities to co-exist. So people are good and bad; ideas are right and wrong; we can worry and be happy. And please understand, I'm not saying it's easy to switch over to this kind of thinking. Here am I espousing it, proselytizing, even; yet all I have to do is read in *Newsweek* a capsule description of one of the new leaders of the new Germany as a "former SS member and television host" and I lose it completely. I become more dualistic than Dr.Jekyll/Mr. Hyde. I start reading the paper like my grandmother: "Jewish/not Jewish; Jewish/not Jewish. Doctor saves boy's life, Jewish. Woman has baby by Satan, not Jewish." But however hard it is, I think it's necessary. In fact, I think the Israelis and the Palestinians are now realizing—in agreeing to renegotiate their boundaries—what it would feel like to approach the issue of boundaries from an and-and point of view. Many of them were quoted the day after the handshake agreement between Arafat and Rabin as saying, "My head worries but my heart is full of hope." So, to approach new ways of defining boundaries means that we first have to renegotiate these closed off boundaries between the heart and the head, rationality and irrationality, subject and object.

Which brings us back again to gender, since in the masculinist ideology that obtains today, men are the rational subjects and women the irrational, hormone-driven objects, men the linear thinkers and women the non-linear, muddled feelers, men the ideal reductionist model, if you believe the medical establishment, who tests drugs only on men because women's bodies are too complex. And again, while I agree wholeheartedly that not only women but the attributes associated with them have for too long been devalued, to the detriment of all, I think the answer is not to celebrate irrationality at the expense of rationality, or to elevate women over men, or to say that women are inherently the one and men the other, but to elevate both men and women and the values attributed to each to equal status, and to reconfigure the continuum as a circle, where both sexes may hop and skip from one part to another in quantum, non-linear fashion.

I realize this conclusion is abstract, to say the least, not to mention far from our common perception of "reality," but there are hopeful signs on the horizon. A football player who recently skipped a game because he wanted to be with his wife when she delivered their child, and the new Miller Beer commercials, which recently switched their ad copy from the either/or "tastes great/less filling" debate to the De Broglie-like "tastes great and less filling" slogan, provide evidence that this kind of thinking can catch on.

And maybe instead of thinking of boundaries in terms of territory to be won or lost, as on the football field or in war or in the boardroom, we can use ballroom dancing as a model. I recently took a ballroom dancing class and found it a humiliating experience because the moment my arms went into the assigned female-partner pose, I was possessed by the dybbuk of my eighth-grade self. I was saying things like, "Oh, no, I think you're a wonderful dancer." "Oh, no, surely that was my fault." "No, it's me, I don't have any rhythm." These are the words of one who has learned to dance backwards, to follow another's lead, not to matter, or to be, as it were, dark matter. It took the teacher's male assistant to set me straight as to just how potent even dark matter can be. He said, "You have to resist more. I can't lead unless you resist." So this is the model I offer, both for those in subservient positions to negotiate their way in these dangerous times, and for those in leadership positions to recognize the importance of their partners, to acknowledge that matter is pulled into shape by the gravitational forces exerted by dark matter, that, in the words of another old song, it takes two to tango.

And now, in the spirit of boundary crossing, let me invite any questions you may have. Because curiosity is the real boundary crosser; being really interested in anything leads you to open doors you never knew were closed in the first place and which might only be closed because you never thought or dared to turn the knob. In the words of Peter H. Richter and Heinz-Otto Peitgen, two scientists who write in the *Morphology of Complex Boundaries*:

The fascination of boundaries lies in their ambivalent role of dividing and connecting at the same time. They mark the transition between different modes of existence. They transmit and control exchange between territories. They are the playground for discovery and conquest.

Only on such a playground will we have an equal playing field.

# Rethinking Success

Panel Discussion

CARRIE MENKEL-MEADOW
MARIA CONTRERAS-SWEET
GERALD J. GIAQUINTA
GARY W. MAXWELL
DOLORES RATCLIFFE
JANICE WOOD

Introduction by Barbara Rosenbaum

As a speaker there are three times you never want to come to the podium. One is after a break, another is after lunch, and the third is after an entertaining and thought-provoking speaker. So I am going to very quickly introduce Carrie Menkel-Meadow, who is the moderator for our panel discussion this afternoon. Carrie is a professor at the UCLA School of Law and has been a co-director of the UCLA Center for the Study of Women as well as a visiting professor at Georgetown University, the University of Toronto, and Stanford Schools of Law. She's won numerous awards for her teaching and legal scholarship. She has an active practice in the area of mediation and alternative dispute resolution, and does ADR mediation training for the Center for Public Resources, Rockwell International, the Bar Association, courts, and private law practices. She's had numerous books, articles, and reviews published, and in her spare time continues her current research, which focuses on the legal profession and education and conflict resolution. It's always a pleasure to introduce someone who is so accomplished, Carrie Menkel-Meadow.

CARRIE MENKEL-MEADOW: Thank you. I share your hesitation in following the act of my good friend Emily Levine. But at the risk of doing so, let me say that we are, in a sense, trying to present the other half of the dualism this afternoon. This morning we heard about some of the research and theory on gender and other issues in the workplace of the 21st Century. This afternoon's panel will talk about what's going on in the real world, shall we say, or as we'll hear about from one of our panelists, the virtual office. So, we'll get a little bit of virtual reality into this session as well.

Our plan was to make this panel interactive, to follow another of Emily's examples, first among ourselves and then with you. This afternoon we will think about some concrete ways in which the workplace might change in the 21st century, following up on some of the dilemmas and the optimistic and pessimistic predictions that were presented this morning. Our question for this panel is, "How do we rethink success in the workplace of the 21st Century?"

What does that mean, success? Researchers have discovered that success means different things to different people. One dualism—and Emily, you can add this to your act—is the notion that men seek hierarchical or vertical satisfaction climbing the corporate or other ladder, while women seek horizontal satisfaction; meaning that, as our State Senator Gary Hart said in his talk, we look for satisfaction in a variety of different spheres of our life. It is important to be successful at work, but it is also important to be successful in other parts of our lives.

One of the first questions I'm going to ask the panelists is to what extent their own workplaces and their own work careers reflect horizontal and/or vertical conceptions of success at work, and how workplaces can be structured so that people can have both vertical and horizontal satisfaction. Another and-and problem. A second question to think about, and I think our panelists will be wonderful exemplars of this, is the extent to which we may not always all be able to be and-and in our very diverse workplaces. We'll talk about how workplaces can call on the different talents of people at different points in their life cycles and at different points in their careers. Why is it that workplaces have to be structured so that everyone has to work in the same way? What are the possible ways that we can construct workplaces so that different people can work in different ways at different points in their lives? These are some of the questions that we want to explore with our panelists. So, without further ado, let me introduce them.

Maria Contreras-Sweet is vice president of the Seven-Up/Royal Crown Bottling Company of Southern California. She has been the head of a number of important organizations, and is currently serving on the Federal Glass Ceiling Commission. She's been very active in local as well as national leadership organizations for women and for Hispanic women.

Gary Maxwell is the human resource manager at the Los Angeles law firm of Irell & Manella, which I learned had 180 lawyers in three offices in the Southern California area. Before that, Gary was a teacher and a principal, so hopefully we'll get to hear about changes in his own work life.

Jerry Giaquinta, the CEO of Bob Thomas & Associates, has had a very extensive career working for Mercedes Benz and Toyota. We are hoping he will bring, along with his other talents, some reflection on international differences in workplace structures.

Janice Wood, is vice president of the Communication Workers of America, District 9. Janice serves as the representative of over 70,000 workers in Nevada, California, and the western region of the CWA. As you can see, we have on the panel representatives of managers, and in the case of Janice, workers. And though our focus thus far today has been on professional and managerial work, it's important to remember why this organization originally got founded—to look at the labor side of things. I'm hoping that Janice will remind us that we need to look not only at those of us who are managing others, but at those of us who are doing a lot of the work that we're talking about reconstructing.

Finally, we have Dolores Ratcliffe, president of the Association of Black Women Entrepreneurs, who herself has had a distinguished career as a small-businesswoman, organizing other small-businesswomen, and teaching in MBA programs in Southern California.

Panelists, how is success defined in your workplace and in your own life, and do these notions of horizontal and vertical satisfaction have any meaning for you?

JANICE WOOD: I would have to say that in my workplace, which for this question means both the labor movement and the telecommunications industry, success, ironically, is defined as the ability to control others. It has little to do with the amount of money you make, how impressive your title is, or how satisfied or happy you are with your work. Those who are seen as successful generally are those who have the ability to control the greatest number of people. At this table at this moment, I would be the most successful because I control the microphone. I control the ability of Jerry and Dolores to speak to you, and you know I don't have the fanciest title. So that, for me, shows us that from the union perspective, union members can never be perceived as successful because we do not have the ability to control anyone but ourselves, and sometimes not always ourselves. Clearly, a thinking person would see that success would be defined as personal satisfaction. But it's never defined in that fashion in either the telecommunications industry or in the labor movement.

MARIA CONTRERAS-SWEET: I went to my dentist the other day and, although this doesn't seem relevant, he asked me, "What are your goals for your teeth? What kind of smile do you want?" And it took me aback because I thought, "What?" And he said, "Well, how do I know if I'm ever successful if I don't know what our goals and your needs are?" And it got me to thinking about how we function at work, and I guess that's why so many of us have spent so much time on these forms that we call PMS (isn't that interesting that we would call them that), Performance Management Systems. At least in my environment, we all define success very differently, and how do we know if we're helping employees be successful if we don't know what their individual needs and goals are? I find that many, many people in our work environment themselves restrict their growth because they'd rather do the vertical things.

We've tried to do some things in response to this. We've tried to do what we call "Value Teams," where we put together teams if we had a crisis, for example. Many of you knew that our company was involved in the aftermath of the Tylenol and Perrier incidents. At the time, we pulled the appropriate HR people, the appropriate marketing people, and the appropriate communications people into a team. And now we find that many of our management decisions are being made by appropriate teams.

So while we're not doing a lot of cross training, we're getting the residual effect of that because we're bringing people together in nontraditional ways to make decisions. And now the economic restrictions on our company (everybody is downsizing) are forcing people to consider how wide they want to go. For example, I used to be solely Public Affairs, and so that meant I hung out in the halls of Sacramento, Carson City, Santa Fe, or D.C. Well, now when our HR people are stuck they'll say, "Maria, help us deal with the minority situation in the company." Or "Maria, since you are accessing the community, can you help us in a marketing program that we're trying to put together?" Declining resources in a company are forcing many of us to rethink whether we want to be vertical or more lateral, which may actually allow us to define our own success.

JERRY GIAQUINTA: I'm running a Marketing Communications Company, a subsidiary of Chiat/Day Advertising. We're probably about 200 people strong. What we're going to be embarking on at the beginning of next year is blowing apart our office structure. There will be no office for a person to come to, and we're not talking about telecommuting. In essence, we're going to the virtual office. We'll redesign our building so that an individual will not have a desk to come to every day, or at least not the same desk. Employees will sign into a work station. It is modeled somewhat after a university, a student union, where employees congregate and interact with each other. There will be a Kinko's production center, a design center, and meeting rooms for clients.

Our feeling is that we don't always get the best ideas with the current 9-to-5 structure. We're in the idea business, basically, and what we do is sell our ideas and mold marketing strategies for our clients. And it's not necessarily between 9 and 5 that you're the brightest or that you come up with the best idea. You could be in the shower at home, you could be anywhere. We feel that about 1/3 of our time might be spent in the office, 1/3 of our time working with the client, and maybe 1/3 of the time at home or wherever our Powerbook or technology will take us.

We don't have titles. I carry a title as it relates to the outside world, but I will sit in any cubicle I can find the same as any other individual, and we will interact in teams, as it relates to the particular client. It might be advertising, PR, or communications teams, and we won't necessarily be working with the same individuals. I think what this does is shift the focus to the work. Those teams that produce the best work or the most creative ideas are those that will be rewarded, usually financially, through getting more business from the client or being able to pay their share of a bonus structure.

Maybe it won't be so important to have a bigger office or bigger title if we have the freedom to do some of our best thinking outside this office structure that was designed in the Industrial Revolution. We feel that technology now allows us to break out of the traditional structure and hierarchy of the office to do what we do best. And I think that is the measure of success—the work product.

DOLORES RATCLIFFE: Being highly pragmatic in the hat that I'm wearing as an entrepreneur, and then somewhat verbally celestial in the hat that I'm wearing as an academic, I can see that these worlds come closer together all the time. People are losing jobs, and we need to be aware of the fact that today's student comes and must come with a variety of skills that haven't been necessary before. Certainly in terms of oral and written communications you must be tops in order to "pitch" or sell yourself, hence your concept about who you are, and what success means to you as an individual, you must be without competition. As an entrepreneur, you provide an alternative resource for looking at the world from a different perspective. I can define the world with an idea, a concept, or a product, and then I must use certain structures in order to make that world a reality.

For example, I was an undergraduate at a university that will go nameless as a communications major with a double minor in Spanish and English. In order to get out of that place, you had to participate in a nearby theater production. The nearby communities were not necessarily overly familiar with someone who looked like me, a young black woman, appearing on their stage. So I called the man on the phone with whom I was to have the audition, and I said—in those days my name was Davis—I said,

"My name is Dolores Davis and I'm to come out to read for the part." He said, "Oh yes, I've heard a lot about you from Professor so-and-so. Are you a blond or are you a brunette?" So I remembered my commitment to get out of that place as quickly and effectively as possible, and I said, "I'm a brunette." So I went out for the reading to a facility that looked very much like the Taj Mahal—it was an old Abbey that had been converted into a theater—and I wandered through this maze of rooms in the hallway and I thought, "Gee, you know, at any moment I could see monks darting out, hooded, in all of their glory." And then I quickly stopped myself because I didn't want to see anything hooded jumping out of anywhere. As I moved forward to the room where the audition was to take place, there were five people seated at a table, and the Robert Redford voice that I had talked with on the phone stood up and said, "May I help you?" And I said, "I'm Dolores Davis, we talked on the phone and I've come to read for the part." And he said, "Oh, yes. I didn't expect you to be so...tall." That, I report to you, is the challenge the contemporary entrepreneur faces: the ability to be flexible under any given set of circumstances.

GARY MAXWELL: It's probably easier in a law firm to identify what success is because law firms without billable hours are like assembly plants without automobiles. That's what drives the law firm. If you don't produce billable hours, you have no revenue. That's one measure. But we're changing that, and the change is mandated by the way clients are willing to pay. They're no longer willing to look at billable hours; rather, they're saying, "If you're going to defend us in this, and if you're going to do this stock offering, then let's arrive at what that's going to be worth to us." And so we see a substantial change in the way the firm is doing business.

We also see a change in the way employees do business. In the 1980s, firms were shopped by the arriving associates, who would calculate what their beginning compensation was going to be, what their moving expenses were going to be, and what bar pay was going to be. They had a list, usually with dollars attached, that created their decision making. Once salaries rose, this very bright group of people never fully realized that what they were doing was selling their souls; because if you're going to ratchet up income, somehow you've got to expect that you're going to have to perform stronger, start faster, and not enjoy the same learning curve that you once did. This held for the support staff as well. When staff saw that beginning attorneys were making $70,000, the secretary who probably knew more about court filing than attorneys did and probably ever will thought, "You know, I'm worth a lot more, too." And so the spiral began. Their lifestyle adjusted to that, and eventually, quality of life became an issue. They suddenly realized that the dollars they were receiving meant that they were working harder and missing something in their life.

We have one associate who graduated at the top of her class from Harvard who decided that what she really wanted to do, and all she had ever really wanted to do before she started law school, was to be a pastry chef. So off she went to work with Wolfgang Puck in the world of pastries. Another associate is off doing work with a cultural center of the arts in Washington, D.C. Suddenly their soul has emerged and they're deciding that it's never a bad thing to have a law degree, but that's not what they want to do with their life.

We're beginning to see that on the staff, too. While secretaries and other staff in a law firm tend to make more money than elsewhere, there are also more demands made of them. They're wondering how to accommodate their needs for family, their needs for going back to school. As I see it, it is not just a gender issue, it's really a quality of life issue. And whether it's a woman, a gay person, a minority, or a white male, the emphasis seems to be coming back to where they can get the satisfaction that balances out their life.

All firms that I know of are working toward accommodating this, but there are limits as to what any employer can do. There are times when it just doesn't make sense to job share, for example. What we have done as a firm when people come in is be very careful to describe what we need and try to elicit from them what they want. For example, we're known as a workaholic law firm, so it's not a good idea for somebody who wants sort of a kicked-back atmosphere to join us because it's not going to be a satisfying environment for them. On the other hand, our benefits director made it very clear before she was hired that she had two kids, that they were probably going to have another one, and that she wanted a job that starts at 7:30 and ends at 3:30. There was just no choice about that as far as she was concerned, and it was worth it for us to accommodate that. What it meant to the firm was that we had to hire an additional clerical-type person who could be there later in the day, because as a 24-hour a day operation, we needed to have somebody who could answer benefits questions after hours. So, though it cost the firm to be able to do it, in the long run, it was worth it. Would we do that for everyone? The answer is no. It depends on the quality of the person, and the firm is judging each of those on the individual qualities of the person and their ability to get the job done. I think that's where priorities are now.

CARRIE MENKEL-MEADOW: I'm about to merge two of the questions and change them a little in light of what we've heard. Jerry's about to have a structure in his organization that is going to use money as the way of building the greatest incentives, and eliminate some of the larger overhead costs and things like offices, prestige, and status that come with a title. And Gary's just told us that Irell and Manella (and they're not alone) have learned that the high compensation race has caused a host of other problems. I'd like to ask the panel what kinds of incentives or measures of success your organizations use, what effects they produce in the workplace, and to what extent they may limit creativity? Obviously, we have an interesting tension between one organization that thinks that by simplifying and by making money the primary and only currency, it will reward creativity and reduce the need for a lot of other things that some people like in their workplace, and a law firm that finds that money is not enough, and that people want other things.

I'd also like to remind the panel that one of our issues is the role of gender in all of this, and in a sense, Jerry, Gary, and others have suggested that some of these questions are not gendered. Picking up on what Joan Acker told us this morning, I wonder whether we might think about whether the incentive systems we choose will wind up having gendered effects that we may not be aware of at the moment. So to put it concretely, Jerry, if someone doesn't have an office to sit in, how will a sick child find their parent?

JERRY GIAQUINTA: Let me start at the beginning. I may have misled you into thinking that we're basing rewards purely on money. What we're trying to do is break workers out of the drudgery of demanding that they be most productive and creative between 9 and 5. That's just not how people work, particularly in our industry, and technology, in a sense, has enabled us to accomplish many of the things that we have been doing in our office outside the office environment. What we do is sit down and create ideas, write, and counsel clients—those are the three components of what we do every day. It's not necessarily true that if I show up at 9 and punch out at 5, all those things are being done most productively. This is not a system based on money. Our goal is to make people the most creative, the most productive, using all the tools at our disposal. If they can do that at home, fine.

If we're able to sell a campaign and idea, that means we're more profitable, and we can give people more money. This is where the money incentive comes in. It's not based on if you come up with this idea, you'll get an extra thousand dollars. We just want to stay employed in a very competitive business. There's a very big shrinkage going on in the L.A. and the national market in our industry, and we want to try to stay out ahead of the curve. But I didn't intend to suggest that money is going to be the carrot: it's breaking out of prison.

Now for the gender issue. Our clients don't care, and I don't care, whether a good marketing or advertising or PR campaign is generated by a man or a woman. We have teams. We're almost 50-50 male-female, and there is no distinction between who can sit in on a writing group. You go with the best idea and try to sell it to your client. I might venture to say we're probably gender-blind in this way. Now, if there's a sick child at home, and an individual comes up with a great idea at home, fine. I don't care where the best idea is born. We really typically don't run into a problem there.

MARIA CONTRERAS-SWEET: I think another important aspect of these questions is that we, as women consumers, undermine our import. In the soft drink industry, we used to get the 7-up cans and fill them with bubbles and some sugar, and if we did that and delivered them back to Ralphs in the appropriate amount of time, we were successful for that day. And at the end of the year people would get their appropriate bonuses. But now we're sensitive to what the public is saying, for example, what kind of containers they want, whether they want bubbles in their water or an Evian-type beverage. And that has resulted in a totally different environment and type of company. Now, not only do we have to be totally on top of our skills inside the company, but we have to be fully aware of what's happening out in the community. How does the hotel industry impact us? If they have a low occupancy rate, what is that going to do to our sales of containers in that industry? Maybe instead of filling as many glass containers for them, with people not traveling, we should distribute more of the plastic two-liter containers. The community's needs are very important to us, and that creates a different culture inside the company.

For employees, that says that you can be as useful outside the company as inside: it's good if you can belong to a group in the evening where you're getting a sense of where the environmental group is going, or where the child care is going, or where legislators are going. One such group just came back and reported to the company about the full set of legislation that Congress passed this year and how many more women's bills—women's issues, family issues—had passed. We try to be informed of what kind of employment environment we're going to have in the company of the future.

I am trying to stress that you and I as consumers have a great deal to say about how a company responds to a community and the kinds of products they deliver, and indirectly, we're helping to create the corporate culture. And so I think it's important that we have groups to send strong messages to corporations. A lot of market-driven companies are responding to the things that we're saying every day, whether we're saying them directly or indirectly by purchasing the product. Our company was receiving a strong environmental message, and so we came up with recycled-content containers. We brought in a whole new department that we would never have had before, a complete extensive environmental department in the company. Again, blind on gender, but it created a new field, a new product line that was determined by our marketing, by our consumer, and the consumer in our business is female.

DOLORES RATCLIFFE: Women are the largest and fastest growing segment of the small business community. Small business is what is driving this country. Small business is what is providing the jobs. In a market where major corporations are downsizing and restructuring positions, people with fantastic skills are propelling small businesses forward. How many people in this room own a television? How many own compact disk players? How many own a portable telephone? How many people in this room own a smart missile? A smart missile? I rest my case: that's where we have been placing our productivity for the last 25 to 30 years in this country. The area that Maria talks about that's driving major corporations in terms of identifying and solving needs also now drives the small business community. We must provide services and jobs where the needs are.

GARY MAXWELL: I think Carrie had asked how we're dealing with the money issue. We're trying to address that by, first of all, being as accommodating as we can on a variety of schedules, or reassigning people if it makes sense to do so, and this is regardless of whether it's a family issue or somebody wanting to go back to school, or somebody having an elder care issue, or some other need to change. The thing that we think will have the most impact for us is finding ways to stimulate employees intellectually and get people involved in the development of things in the firm.

For example, we have some secretaries who were eager to develop a litigation-secretarial handbook. Now, within the next two months, every litigation secretary is going to have this notebook. It would have been a deathlike assignment to me—I would have cut off my right hand to avoid doing it. But they loved it, and they're making a terrific contribution to the firm. You see, as paralegals entered the market, they took away a lot of the exciting things that secretaries did. Secretaries and attorneys used to be this team that together would put together a deal, and do a court filing. Then the legal assistants came in, and these tended to be women too. It was a time when not as many women were going to law school, and this provided sort of a good bridge. And while they're critical to the well-being of the firm, what we're trying to do is get more of the intellectual stuff back to the legal secretaries because they are a very bright group.

JANICE WOOD: Two things seem to be happening at the same time. One is the thing that you referred to, Maria, where people don't want to be together. They don't want to know each other, they don't want to deal with each other because they see or hear some difference. At the same time, I see that corporations are very excited about the possibility of telecommuting and moving work electronically to people rather than moving people to work. So we have people who don't want to be together, and we have the ability to provide them with the opportunity to stay totally apart and never have to interact in any way. I don't think that's good for people, and I don't think that's good for society, and I think it's happening. And I don't think anybody's concerned about it. It looks very good, because you don't have to clog up the freeway with your car. But nobody considers all of the other things that go along with that. I particularly don't think it's good for women who, as Emily said earlier, are here but not really included yet in the decision making that goes on in the workplace. And so what I'm wondering is, is there anybody else who worries that we have the ability to keep people apart and the will that we see growing to stay apart?

GARY MAXWELL: I sort of sense that the thing that keeps people apart is an overemphasis on the special interest group to the point where the special interest groups are almost competing with one another, when in actuality their intent is to accommodate diversity. And I think that a lot of the goals of women are not that different from the goals of most other minority-status people. Being a gay male, being way over 50, and with a minor handicap, I find myself trying to figure out what camp I want to go into. Do I want to fight for the rights of the aging, do I want to fight for gay rights—what's fair? And how do we accommodate everybody? If only 10 or 15 percent of any organization is white male, some of it will still be male, some of it may even, God forbid, be gay, but we all have the same goal, and if we could work together in presenting a common front, employers could focus on that.

This was an important issue for me when I interviewed. Having come out of Education, where you could be booted out of schools for being gay, I wanted to know that my partner would be welcome to come to firm functions and that I didn't have to pretend like my partner was a woman. I think that the issues are very common among groups and that we need to work toward getting everybody represented in that diversity.

DOLORES RATCLIFFE: I certainly would concur with that, but I think that Emily said it very well when she talked about duality. That's what you're sensing, Janice, and that's what we all sense. The duality of the technology that will allow us to have home-based businesses and stay off the cluttered freeways, and the need for us to support one another in our common efforts. That's a reality, and I've grown to accept it. I realize that there's going to be duality: the duality of a world that looks at immigration and the founding of this country as a marvelous experience, but immigration of a different type of people in a different century as very detrimental; the duality of living in an environment that values the display of material success and that also says we must smell the roses, respect the environment, and look at those things that are naturally made. I've adjusted to duality.

JANICE WOOD: But let me ask you this, and maybe it's because I don't work with professionals or academics for the most part, but most of the men I know don't know what they would do all day if they didn't work. And most of the women I know do know what they would do all day if they didn't work. And so what I'm frightened of is that the ability to stay at home will be more seductive to women because they will see that there will be more time and opportunity to do those things that they would be doing if they weren't working. Where men want to get up and say, "Get me out of the house and get me to the job." And so my fear is that women will become more and more isolated, that we will simply slide farther and farther back away from the progress that we've made in the workplace and that we will again become the homebodies that we were before World War II.

JERRY GIAQUINTA: I'd like to ask a question. How many of you look forward to the next 20-25 years going into an office, including commuting time, from 7:30 to 6 p.m.? Is that something you set as a personal goal, something that would be rewarding to you, whether it was a wonderful place or a horrible place?

DOLORES RATCLIFFE: Since I have the microphone, I have the power. I wouldn't relish it, Jerry, and I don't intend to have as one of my goals that type of commuting.

MARIA CONTRERAS-SWEET: But you know what, they're not mutually exclusive. What I find now when I serve on a corporate board is people saying, "We've done a lot of studies, we want to be responsive to the new work life, and downtown Los Angeles may not be the best place for our building. It may be that we need to have a more campus-style building out somewhere where there is an opportunity to do some development and build some moderate housing. And elevators are not very efficient—you lose a lot of time moving up and down the 32 floors of that building, and so we need to wipe elevators out." And so I don't know that's it's always going to be 9 to 5, but I think we're going to find a different campus-style company in the future. Many of us have equipment at home. In fact my lobbyist the other day said to me. "Maria you're taking my time away from me." I said "What do you mean, your time?" He said, "My time to think. I used to drive to work and that was my thinking time, that was the most important time of my day, and now, you got me the car phone so I can't think because you can call me anytime you want in the car. And then my time to think became after I parked my car until the time I walked into the office, but now you've gotten me a portable phone and the phone is with me all the time, and I am concerned about that—I don't have any time to think anymore." And I thought that was a very provocative statement because I think we have to reevaluate the 9-to-5 day and how we spend our time, when we get to think. It's almost as if we have to put things on our calendar that we might have not thought about before.

JERRY GIAQUINTA: I don't think we need fear the fact that technology might allow us to do certain functions away from that block of time that we call the office. And I think that's where I might disagree with you. I don't think it will keep women in their place. As a matter of fact, in our industry, I think the best ideas will come forth, and if they come forth at home, it's really not a gender issue.

AUDIENCE QUESTION: I read in the paper recently that 85 percent of women in the workplace would prefer to work for a man rather than a woman.

JANICE WOOD: I don't believe for a moment that 85 percent of the women in the workplace have ever worked for a woman. Once every woman has that opportunity, maybe those figures will change.

MARIA CONTRERAS-SWEET: I'm delighted that you raised that question. Early on women started moving toward the glass ceiling, and then, you know, we hit the ceiling and got the concussion. Incidentally, I wear the pin of Izzy and Shimonoya showing the glass ceiling, and if you don't know about it, I'll tell you about it later. But I think in the beginning when there were very few women in corporations, those women had a tremendous need to be superwomen, and I think that there was a lot of what you said going on because there was this concern about, "I must be the best. I must be fabulous. I have to be tougher than the men, I have to be, and I especially have to be tougher on women, or people of my same gender." As more women have moved into that arena we've become more relaxed with who we are in that role, even with all the things that we really shoulder.

We now see women going out and saying, "Hey, I'm leaving next year. I want to groom you to take my place." And I think that's the kind of thinking we must do as women, as men, as responsible workers. But I do tend to think, as I think back on some things, that women did suffer, a few of them, with that whole need to be mucho macha. And we've moved from that, thank goodness.

GARY MAXWELL: The executive director of our firm is a woman, and it's not a matter of a glass ceiling. It's just unless she gets a J.D., she's not going to go any further. But probably the best successes I've had have been working with women, and it would be surprising to me that that feeling would be held. I would agree that it's probably a residue of maybe an earlier generation where women had to fight so hard to get through that they had a different persona. They were all wearing two piece suits with silk blouses then, too, and that was because women were discouraged from wearing a silk dress, like they would normally do. It made no sense. I think today's women executives are much different.

MARIA CONTRERAS-SWEET: One of the things that we have found, however, in our research on the glass ceiling is that, while we have had some success bringing women in, some of us have been reluctant to nurture the others—to say, "Well, now it's my responsibility, since someone did something incredibly wonderful to get me in here, to reciprocate and bring in three more." In one company, 40 percent of officers were female, yet the pipeline didn't reflect that. We looked into it and finally got a commitment from the top to maintain that percentage despite the fact that the pipeline coming in is not representative of that. We need to nurture others so that the pool is always full.

Contributors

JOAN ACKER, Professor, Department of Sociology, University of Oregon. B.A., Hunter College, N.Y.; M.A., University of Chicago; Ph.D., University of Oregon. Formerly: Research Professor, the Swedish Center for Working Life, Stockholm, Sweden 1987-89; Director, Center for the Study of Women in Society, University of Oregon 1982-86; Director, Center for the Sociological Study of Women, University of Oregon 1973-81. Since 1969 she has held several visiting scholar appointments in Norway, Finland, Toronto, Sweden, and England. She has authored, edited, or reviewed numerous articles and papers, particularly on women's issues. Editorial Board, *Economic and Industrial Democracy* and *Gender, Organizations and Work*. Consultant, Work Research Institute, Trondheim, Norway. Consultant, Women and Work Project, Tampere University, Tampere, Finland. Associate Editor, *Gender and Society*. Member: American Sociological Association; Sociologists for Women in Society; International Sociological Association; and Pacific Sociological Association. In 1993 she was honored with the American Sociological Association's Award for a Career of Distinguished Scholarship.

MARIA CONTRERAS-SWEET, Vice President, Seven-Up/RC Bottling Company of Southern California. She was the first woman elected President of the powerful California Nevada Soft Drink Association. Member, Board of Directors and Executive Committee of Blue Cross of California. She was recently elected to the Board of Governors of Town Hall of California. Commissioner on the Los Angeles County Commission for Women; Regent at Loyola Marymount University; and Member of the Children's Bureau of Southern California. She currently is a U.S. Senate appointee to the Federal Glass Ceiling Commission, and chairs the Health, Human Services and Youth Programs Task Force for Rebuild L.A. (RLA). She is the founding President of HOPE (Hispanas Organized for Political Equality). Her priorities are women and children, education, the environment, and political education and empowerment. She has received numerous awards, including "Woman of the Year" during the National Hispanic Women's Conference and "Humanitarian of the Year" from the Rossi Youth Foundation.

GERALD J. GIAQUINTA, President and Chief Executive Officer, Bob Thomas & Associates. BT&A is among the six largest public relations and marketing communications agencies in Southern California. B.A., University of Massachusetts; Ph.D., University of Southern California; J.D., Loyola Law School. Board of Directors, School of Public Administration, University of Southern California. Board of Directors, California Council on International Trade 1983-85. Regional Vice-President/Executive Committee, Mercedes-Benz of North America, Montvale, N.J. 1989-92. National Car Advertising Manager, Toyota Motor Sales, USA, Los Angeles 1980-89. Media Relations Associate, Eli Lilly and Company, Indianapolis 1977-80.

JUDITH GLASS, Coordinator of Public Programs, Center for Human Resource Management, Institute of Industrial Relations, UCLA. B.A., Barnard College, Columbia University; M.A., New York University; Ph.D., UCLA. Prior experience includes college teaching; development and administration of an MBA in not-for-profit management, directing the Interfaith Center to Reverse the Arms Race, and Institute for the Study of Women and Men at the University of Southern California. She participated in two National Endowment for the Humanities seminars on teaching the social history of American women. She is consultant to community organizations on strategic planning and feminist issues. She is the author of several articles on feminism, ethics and economics, and unionization of farm workers, as well as a workbook for students on job choice entitled *Whose Bread You Eat Their Song You'll*

Sing. At the Institute, she is currently responsible for the ongoing project on the Dynamics of Gender in the Workplace.

GARY K. HART, State Senator, California. His district (the 18th) includes portions of Santa Barbara, San Luis Obispo, Ventura and Los Angeles Counties. Served eight years in the State Assembly and has just completed his tenth year of service in the State Senate. B.A., Stanford University; M.A., Harvard University. He is a former teacher and recognized as one of the key educational leaders in California. He has served as the Chairman of the Senate Education Committee since 1983; Vice Chair of the Senate Natural Resources Committee. He is a member of the Committees on Budget & Fiscal Review, Energy & Public Utilities, Business & Professions, and Constitutional Amendments. He has authored SB 1274 which created more than 150 "restructured schools" committed to developing innovative ways to deliver educational services. Also authored SB 1448 which authorizes the creation of charter schools. He has played an important role in other issues key to children's lives. In 1991 he authored a major reform of the child support system that resulted in raising child support awards and increasing enforcement efforts to ensure that those who are supposed to pay support do so. He was also instrumental in establishing the "latchkey" child care program and authored legislation creating a child care tax credit for employers who provide care for their employees' children. He has taken the lead in environmental issues as well. His strong environmental record led the Planning and Conservation League to name him California's 1990 "Environmental Legislator of the Year."

EMILY LEVINE, Writer/Comedian/Philosopher. Graduate, Harvard University. She was a member of the improvisational comedy group, the "New York City Stickball Team." She appeared on stage, in a one-woman show, "Myself, Myself, I'll Do It Myself," which she wrote and performed herself. This led her to the world of stand-up comedy. She has also written and performed an Emmy-award-winning series of commercial satire segments for WNET in New York; served as Executive Script Consultant on such television series as "Angie" and "The Associates"; and written two screenplays, "Fast and Furious" for MGM-UA and "Snatched" for Goldie Hawn and Warner Brothers. From 1982 to 1989, she was partnered, first with Universal Studios, then with the Walt Disney Company, as an independent writer/producer responsible for creating, writing, and producing new situation comedies for network television. She has written Op-Ed for the *Los Angeles Times*. In 1991 she was producer on the first season of the television show "Room for Two." She was also the head writer on the television show "Designing Women." She is currently developing new pilots for the 1994 television season and honing a work-in-progress called "Chaos/Paradox/Ballroom Dancing."

GARY W. MAXWELL, Administrative Director, Irell & Manella, a 180-attorney law firm based in Century City, California. Included among his other responsibilities with the firm are recruiting and human resources functions. He has been involved with the Association of Legal Administrators at the local and national levels. He is also involved with the local and national recruiting organizations. B.S., California State University, Long Beach; M.Ed., Loyola University. He taught and was principal at elementary schools in the Santa Monica School District, Santa Monica, California, for 16 years. He also spent two years teaching college in Honolulu.

CARRIE J. MENKEL-MEADOW, Professor of Law, UCLA Law School. A.B., Barnard College, Columbia University; J.D., University of Pennsylvania Law School. Acting Co-Director, UCLA Center for the Study of Women 1989-90. Visiting Professor of Law, Georgetown University Law Center, Fall 1992, Spring 1994. Distinguished Visiting Professor in Legal Theory, University of Toronto Law Faculty, Fall 1990. Visiting Professor, Stanford Law School, Fall 1990. Arbitrator, Dalkon Shield Claims Trust, 1992 to present. Mediator: Lawyer's Mediation Service 1991 to present; L.A. and Santa Monica Municipal and Superior Courts; Asbestos Claims Facility 1988 to present. Trainer, Center for Public Resources, Legal & Corporate Alternative Dispute Resolution. Mediation

Trainer, U.S. District Court for Northern California 1993. She has authored numerous books, monographs, articles, and book chapters. Bar admissions: Pennsylvania 1974; U.S. District Court, E.D. Pa. 1974; U.S. Third Circuit Court of Appeals 1975; California 1979. She is doing on-going comparative research on women in the legal profession.

DOLORES RATCLIFFE, Founder/President, Executive Board, Association of Black Women Entrepreneurs. President, Corita Communications, Inc., Intec (International Technical Educational Consultants). Corita Communications was established in 1979; its clients include, among others, ARCO, Pacific Bell, Women Construction Owners and Executives, UCLA Materials Department, the Southern California Gas Company, Asian Business Association and Los Angeles Urban League. Has written and published five books through her company. Active in the business community. Serves on the Executive Boards of Pacific Coast Regional Small Business Development Corporation; Region 9, U.S. Small Business Administration; Southwest Rotary International; Black Women Entrepreneurs. Has been quoted or featured in: *The Wall Street Journal; USA Today; Female Executive; Entrepreneurial Woman;* and many radio and television shows, including a recent taping on the Oprah Winfrey Show.

JULIET B. SCHOR, Senior Lecturer on Economics, Harvard University, and Director of Studies, Women's Studies, Harvard University. B.A., Wesleyan University. Ph.D., University of Massachusetts. Associate Professor of Economics, Harvard University, March 1989 to June 1992. Head Tutor, Committee on Degrees in Women's Studies, Harvard University, July 1991 to June 1992. Research Advisor, Project on Global Macropolicy, World Institute for Development Economics Research (WIDER), United Nations, August 1985 to March 1992. Assistant Professor of Economics, Harvard University, July 1984 to March 1989. Assistant Professor of Economics, Barnard College, Columbia University 1983-84. Assistant Professor of Economics, Williams College 1981-83. She has written numerous books, articles, and papers, most recently, *The Overworked American,* winner of numerous book awards. She is currently doing a project on gender differences in consumption behavior. Editorial Board, *International Journal of Applied Economics,* August 1992 to present. Standing Committee on South Asian Studies, Harvard University, July 1991 to present. Standing Committee on Women's Studies, Harvard University, July 1989 to present. Economic Columnist, *Z* magazine, December 1987 to present. Research Affiliate, Center for European Studies, Harvard University, July 1986 to present. Research Advisory Council, Economic Policy Institute, September 1986 to present.

JANICE WOOD, Vice President, Communications Workers of America District Nine. Elected CWA District Nine Vice President in April 1992. Represents approximately 70,000 workers in California, Nevada, and Hawaii. She was previously President of CWA Local 9000 in Los Angeles for ten years. Member of the Executive Council of the California State AFL-CIO.